BOOSEY'S
GUIDE TO THE OPERA

CONTAINING

THE PLOTS AND INCIDENTS OF

ALL THE BEST KNOWN OPERAS PERFORMED IN ENGLAND,

WITH SHORT SKETCHES OF THE LIVES OF THE COMPOSERS,
&c., &c.

EDITED BY

ALFRED SCOTT GATTY.

NEW EDITION PREPARED BY

NICHOLAS GATTY.

British Library Cataloguing-in-Publication Data
A catalogue record for this book is available from
the British Library

Singing

Singing is the act of producing musical sounds with the voice, and augments regular speech by the use of both tonality and rhythm. In many respects, human song is a form of sustained speech – accompanied by a rich plethora of cultural associations and a unique history of its own. Singing can be formal or informal, arranged or improvised. It may be done for pleasure, comfort, ritual, education, or profit. Excellence in singing may require time, dedication, instruction, and regular practice – but when composed and performed well, is one of the most immediate, and beautiful forms of artistic communication we have.

In its physical aspect, singing has a well-defined technique that depends on the use of the lungs, which act as an air supply, or bellows; on the larynx, which acts as a reed or vibrator; on the chest and head cavities, which have the function of an amplifier, as the tube in a wind instrument; and on the tongue, which together with the palate, teeth, and lips articulate and impose consonants and vowels on the amplified sound. Though these four mechanisms function independently, they are nevertheless coordinated in the establishment of a vocal technique and are made to interact upon one another.

The sound of each individual's singing voice is entirely unique not only because of the actual shape and size of an individual's vocal cords but also due to the size and shape of the rest of that person's body. Humans have vocal folds which can loosen, tighten, or change their thickness, and over which breath can be transferred at varying pressures. The shape of the chest and neck, the position of the tongue, and the tightness of otherwise unrelated muscles can be altered. Any one of these actions results in a change in pitch, volume, timbre, or tone of the sound produced. Sound also resonates within different parts of the body and an individual's size and bone structure can affect the sound produced.

Singers can also learn to project sound in certain ways so that it resonates better within their vocal tract. This is known as vocal resonation. Another major influence on vocal sound and production is the function of the larynx which people can manipulate in different ways to produce different sounds. These different kinds of laryngeal function are described as different kinds of vocal registers. Each of these vibratory patterns appears within a particular range of pitches and produces certain characteristic sounds. In addition to vocal registers, singers also have to be aware of vocal resonation – the process by which the basic product of phonation is enhanced in timbre and/or intensity by the air-filled cavities through which it passes on its way to the outside air. There are seven areas that may be listed as possible vocal resonators including the chest, the tracheal tree, the larynx itself, the pharynx, the oral cavity, the nasal cavity and the sinuses.

In European classical music and opera, voices are treated like musical instruments. Composers who write vocal music must have an understanding of the skills, talents, and vocal properties of singers. Most classical music systems acknowledge seven different major voice categories. Women are typically divided into three groups: soprano, mezzo-soprano, and contralto. Men are usually divided into four groups: countertenor, tenor, baritone, and bass. When considering voices of pre-pubescent children an eighth term, treble, can be applied. Within each of these major categories there are several sub-categories that identify specific vocal qualities like coloratura facility (referring to elaborate melodies in operatic singing – coming out of the eighteenth and nineteenth century operatic tradition – with runs, trills, wide leaps or similar virtuoso-like material) and vocal weight to differentiate between voices.

A further important classification in singing technique, is the difference between 'chest voice' and 'head voice' – a distinction first made in the thirteenth century by the writers Johannes de Garlandia and Jerome of Moravia. The terms were later adopted within *bel canto*, the Italian operatic singing method, where chest voice was identified as the lowest and head voice the highest of three vocal registers: the chest, passagio and head registers. This approach is still taught by some vocal pedagogists today. As knowledge of physiology has increased over the past two hundred years however, so has the understanding of the physical process of singing and vocal production. As a result, many vocal pedagogists have redefined or even abandoned the use of the terms chest voice and head voice. In particular, the use of the terms *chest register* and *head register* have become controversial since vocal registration is more commonly seen today as a product of laryngeal function that is unrelated to the physiology of the chest, lungs, and head.

Vocal music is probably the oldest form of music, since it does not require any instrument besides the voice. All musical cultures have some form of vocal music, and there are many and varied long standing singing traditions all over the globe. Vocal music is written in many different forms and styles, which are often labelled within a particular genre of music. These genres include: Art music, Popular music, Traditional music, regional and national music, and fusions of those genres. Within these larger genres are many subgenres. For example, popular music would encompass blues, jazz, country music, easy listening, hip hop, rock music, and several other genres. There may also be a subgenre within a subgenre, such as vocalese and scat singing in jazz.

One difference between 'popular' live performances and the classical genres is that whereas classical performers often sing without amplification in small to mid-size halls, in popular music, a microphone and PA system (amplifier and speakers) are used in almost all performance venues, even a small coffee house. The use of the microphone has had several impacts on popular music. For one, it facilitated the development of intimate, expressive singing styles such as 'crooning' which would not have enough projection and volume if done without a microphone. As well, pop singers who use microphones can do a range of other vocal styles that would not project without amplification, such as making whispering sounds, humming, and mixing half-sung and sung tones. As well, some performers use the microphone's response patterns to create effects, such as bringing the microphone very close to the mouth to get an enhanced bass response, or, in the case of hip-hop beatboxers, doing plosive "p" and "b" sounds into the microphone to create percussive effects.

As is evident from this very brief introduction to the art of singing, it is a field of human endeavour with an incredibly long history. Singing is enjoyed by cultures all over the world, and it encompasses an enormous array of skill, imagination and hard-work – practiced solo, or as part of a choir, band, or whole community. It is hoped that the current reader enjoys this book on the subject.

INTRODUCTION.

In placing this small work before the public, the Editor hopes to supply a want felt by most opera-goers. But few of us are sufficiently well acquainted with foreign languages to be able to gather the story of an opera from hearing the words sung at the theatre; our only chance, therefore, is to follow every line with the translations of the libretti we buy *en route* to, or in, the theatre; but as this keeps the eyes constantly on the book, and but seldom on the stage, the best part of the performance is lost to us. This little volume contains all the well-known operas, arranged in the form of short narratives. Two minutes' reading before the curtain rises will enable the playgoer to know all the leading incidents of the piece in the order that they will occur; thus, instead of having to keep his eyes upon a book, he will be able to devote both eyes and ears exclusively to the stage.

To those who attend the opera as students our little book does not apply, as they are already so well provided for in the most part by Messrs. Boosey & Co.'s admirable "Royal Edition."

It is hoped that the short sketches of the lives of the composers, and the footnotes appended to these short analyses, may help towards an intelligent enjoyment of the operas, and may even prove of interest to the general reader.

London, April, 1880.   THE EDITOR.

Since this book first appeared it is obvious that many changes have had to be made. Old favourites have had to be removed to make room for the many works of the modern Italian school and the later music-dramas of Wagner, &c. In the process of excision only those operas which seem to have completely fallen into oblivion have been dealt with. The selection has not been an easy matter, but it will be found that there are many operas left in which, though they have not been heard in London for a long time, are so famous that their revival is a matter of reasonable expectation.

April, 1908.   N. G.

INDEX.

AUBER.

DANIEL FRANÇOIS ESPRIT AUBER was born at Caen, in Normandy, on Jan. 29th, 1782, during a visit that his parents made to that town. His father was a printseller in Paris. Wishing his son to devote himself to business, he sent him to London ; but Auber, becoming disgusted with a career so utterly adverse to all his tastes, returned to Paris, and there was soon well known as a song or ballad writer. His first attempt in writing for the stage was made in 1813, in the one-act opera, entitled " Le Séjour Militaire," which was produced at the Théâtre Feydeau, and met with but a poor reception. During his career he was made Commander of the Legion of Honour, and received the decoration of the Belgian Order of Leopold. He died May 12th-13th, 1871.

FRA DIAVOLO.*

THE scene of this opera is laid near Terracina, in Italy. Fra Diavolo, the brigand, passing himself off as the Marquis of San Marco, has been following through Italy Lord Rocburg, an English nobleman, and the Lady Pamela, his wife, having in view the abduction of the lady, who is vain and foolish, and the robbery of their baggage, which is large and valuable.

In the opening scene a band of Carbineers are feasting outside a village inn, preparatory to starting in chase of Fra Diavolo and his followers. Lorenzo, their captain, is in love with Zerlina, the daughter of Matteo, the innkeeper, but has been refused by her father as a suitor on account of his poverty, and on the morrow she is about to marry a rich young farmer called Francesco. Lorenzo is about bidding his ladylove farewell,

---

* Was produced at the Opéra Comique, Paris, Jan. 28th, 1830 ; and in London, Nov. 3rd, 1831. Mlle. Zare Thalberg caused a great sensation in the year 1875 by her rendering of the character of Zerlina in this opera. A daughter of the celebrated pianist, she was born at New York, April 15th, 1858, and made her *début* at Covent Garden, April 10th, 1875.

when Lord and Lady Rocburg enter, who describe how they have been robbed by the brigands a short distance from the inn, and his Lordship offers 10,000 francs reward for the recovery of his property. Lorenzo hurries off with his men in pursuit of the robbers.

Fra Diavolo, as the Marquis of San Marco, arrives, much to the chagrin of Lord Rocburg and to the delight of his lady. He takes a bed at the inn, and anon two of his companions, Beppo and Giacomo, come and ask for a supper and bed, proclaiming themselves pilgrims ; for these the Marquis pays. The last scene of this Act is the re-entrance of Lorenzo, victorious, having encountered the brigands and regained the stolen property. Lady Pamela hands him the 10,000 francs.

The scene of the second Act is Zerlina's bedchamber ; she leaves to show Lord Rocburg and his lady their room, and, while absent, the Marquis enters her room with his two companions, intent upon plundering the English lord. Hearing Zerlina returning, they hide in a cupboard. She commences her night toilet, and, being tired, falls asleep over her prayers. The three brigands then creep out, and Beppo is about to stab Zerlina, but is deterred by her murmuring the Virgin's name in her sleep ; he is about a second time to plunge the dagger into her, when a loud knocking and shouting is heard outside. The robbers again hide in the cupboard, and Zerlina, opening her window, finds that her lover Lorenzo is without with his companions. She throws him the key of the house, and he enters ; she then goes out to get refreshments for him and his followers, leaving him and Lord Rocburg, who has been disturbed in his slumbers, in her room. They hear a noise in the cupboard, and are about to open the door, when out steps the Marquis, who tells them that he had clandestine appointments with both Lady Pamela and Zerlina. Lorenzo, in despair at Zerlina's implied unfaithfulness, arranges to meet the Marquis the following morning at seven in mortal combat. On this Lady Pamela and Zerlina appear, who are at a loss to understand the situation, neither of them being in any way concerned in the presence of the Marquis.

The last Act opens with Fra Diavolo, as the Marquis, explaining how he has planted an ambush for Lorenzo, and writing instructions on a piece of paper for Beppo and Giacomo, which he places in the hollow trunk of a tree, and leaves. Beppo and Giacomo find the paper, which tells them that as soon as Lorenzo is murdered, the Carbineers sent off on the wrong scent, and the people of the inn gone to the wedding feast, they are to ring the Hermitage bell and he will come and seize Lady Pamela and the booty. Hearing steps approach, they retire, and the villagers assemble for the wedding feast. Matteo is about to join the hands of Zerlina and Francesco, when she breaks away, and running to Lorenzo, begs him to save her and to tell her why he shuns her. He refuses. On this Beppo and Giacomo make fun of her, describing the scene in the bedroom, and how she said certain things to herself. Zerlina says she does not know how they obtained their knowledge, and begs Lorenzo to find out. He orders the soldiers to seize them, and on Giacomo is found the paper containing Fra Diavolo's instructions. Acting under Lorenzo's orders, all hide except Beppo, who is made to act as decoy. The Hermitage bell is rung, and Fra Diavolo enters, thinking the coast is clear; but he is immediately surrounded, and Lorenzo, having won the reward offered for his head, is able to come forward and be accepted as the suitor of Zerlina.

BEETHOVEN.

LUDWIG VAN BEETHOVEN was a son of one Johann van Beethoven, a tenor singer in the Chapel of the Elector at Cologne, and grandson of Ludwig van Beethoven, singer, and afterwards Master, of the same chapel. He was born at Bonn on the Rhine on Dec. 16th, 1770, and commenced at the early age of five to learn music under his father. His first regular musical instructor, however, was Van den Eeden, organist to the Court, but he, dying in 1782, was succeeded by Neefe, who continued the instruction of Beethoven. On Dec. 18th, 1792, his father died, and Beethoven was sent by the Elector of Cologne to finish his musical education under the then celebrated Joseph Haydn, but on the latter's departure for England, two years afterwards, he was placed under the care of the learned Albrechtsberger. Beethoven never married, though his most intimate friend, Dr. Wegeler, says of him that he was always in love. During the latter years of his life he was stone deaf, and dying of dropsy on March 26th, 1827, at Vienna, was buried in the cemetery of Wahring, near that city. His one opera is—

FIDELIO,*

The scene of which is laid in one of the State prisons of Spain. Pizarro, governor of the prison, has unjustly incarcerated Florestan Fernando, against whom he has the most inveterate hatred. Leonora, his wife, adopting male attire and taking the name of Fidelio, gets taken into the service of Rocco, head gaoler of the prison. Thus disguised, she is fallen in love with by Marcellina, the gaoler's daughter, much to the chagrin of Jacquino, Rocco's assistant, who is in love with Marcellina. It is here that Act I. begins with a duet, in which Marcellina repulses the advances of Jacquino. Marcellina but too soon forgets her old love for the new, and her father determines to ask Pizarro's consent to make Fidelio his assistant gaoler and son-in-law. Pizarro receives a missive from the Minister to say that he intends making a surprise visit to the prison, as he hears that many persons are being unjustly kept incarcerated. Pizarro, acting on the old saying "Dead men tell no tales," determines to murder Florestan, and having given consent to Fidelio acting as under-

---

* This opera was first produced at Vienna in the autumn of the year 1805 ; in Paris, May 5th, 1860; in London, May 18th, 1832; and in an English version with Malibran, June 12th, 1835.

gaoler and to his marriage with Marcellina, he orders Rocco to prepare a grave for Florestan. On the King's birthday Fidelio begs Rocco to let the prisoners walk for a short time in the prison garden, in the hopes of seeing her husband among them, but he does not appear. Pizarro is very angry, and orders the prisoners back to their cells, but forgives Rocco and Fidelio on their going to dig the grave.

In the second Act Florestan is discovered in his dungeon. After bewailing his wretched fate, he falls asleep, exhausted. Rocco and Fidelio enter with spade and mattock to dig his grave; while they are at work Florestan awakes, and on his speaking to Rocco, Fidelio, or Leonora, recognizes her husband, but has to restrain herself: anon Pizarro enters, wrapt in a cloak and armed with a dagger. Ordering Fidelio to leave, he is about to stab Florestan, when Fidelio rushes in between them, and, covering Pizarro with a pistol, bid him defiance. At this moment a blast of trumpets announces the arrival of the Minister, and Pizarro has to leave to attend to him. The scene changes, and the Minister ordering all the prisoners to be released, bids Leonora with her own hands set her husband at liberty, promising to visit Pizarro's treacherous behaviour as it deserves.

BELLINI.

VINCENZO BELLINI was born on Nov. 1st, 1801, at Catania, the capital of Sicily; he was son and grandson of musicians of small repute. In 1819 he was admitted to the conservatory of music at Naples. He studied counterpoint under Tritto and Zingarelli. His first opera, "Ade.son e Salvina," was produced in 1825 at the small theatre attached to the Royal College of Music. His next work was "Bianca e Fernando," which was produced at the Theatre San Carlo on June 30th, 1826. In 1827 his "Pirata" was performed at Milan, in which Rubini, the great tenor, took the principal *rôle*. This was followed in 1829 by "La Straniera," Mme. Meric Lalande and Tamburini both taking part in it, and no doubt greatly assisting in the success which it had. Bellini died at Paris, from some internal disorder, on Sept. 24th, 1835.

NORMA.*

THE scene opens at night in a sacred forest of the Druids and Temple of Irminsul in Gaul. Norma, the daughter of the Archdruid Orovero, with much pomp cuts the sacred mistletoe and prophesies the downfall of Rome. The district is under the government of Pollio, a Roman pro-consul, the Roman armies having overrun the country. Unknown to any one but her friend Clotilda, Norma has been untrue to her vows, and is the mother of two children, of whom Pollio is the father. But Pollio transfers his affections to another young priestess, Adalgisa, who returns his love and is under a promise to fly with him to Rome. She tells her story in confidence to Norma, who thereupon discovers Pollio's faithless-ness, and the first Act closes with a scene between her, Adalgisa, and Pollio, in which Norma threatens him with her vengeance.

Distracted with grief and rage, Norma is on the point of murdering her two children, but her mother-instinct prevails, and she seeks con-solation from Adalgisa. The latter endeavours to induce Pollio to return to his first love, Norma, but he is infatuated, and will have nothing but the new object of his affection. Norma summons the Druids to arms,

----

* Was composed at Milan in the year 1831, and produced on Dec. 26th of the same year; was first heard in London, at the King's Theatre, June 20th, 1833.

and suddenly Pollio is brought in by the Gauls, having been found lurking in the temple devoted to the priestesses. The Gauls demand his life as the victim for the altar before going to war. Norma hesitates, and offers him his freedom if he promises to renounce Adalgisa. This he wi not do. She threatens Adalgisa's life with as little success, on which, in a scene of much power, Norma finally denounces herself as a perjured priestess and mother, commends her children to Clotilda's care, offers herself as the victim, and ascends the sacrificial pile. Overcome at her noble conduct, Pollio's old affection is re-awakened, and he shares her fate on the funeral pyre.

Là più puro, là più santo,
Incomincia eterno amor !

I PURITANI.*

THIS opera is founded upon an incident supposed to have taken place during the English civil war of Roundheads and Cavaliers. The scene is laid at a fortress near Plymouth, of which Lord Walter Walton is the Puritan governor. He has under his care a female prisoner, supposed to be an emissary of the Stuart cause, but who is none other than Henrietta, the widow of Charles I. The governor had promised the hand of his daughter Elvira to Sir Richard Foster, a Puritan colonel, but she being in love with Lord Arthur Talbot, a Cavalier, her uncle, Sir George Walton, pleads her cause with her father, and secures his consent to her being allowed to refuse the addresses of the colonel and accept Talbot as her future husband.

All is prepared for their nuptials, and Lord Arthur comes laden with bridal presents ; Henrietta manages to tell him who she is, and how she has been summoned to appear before the Parliament in London, where-upon he determines somehow to effect her escape. Elvira, entering with her bridal veil, and wishing to see how it will look, throws it over Henrietta. Suddenly the idea strikes Lord Arthur that he can pass her off as his bride, and by this means effect her escape from the castle. Elvira, on hearing of their flight, thinking her lover untrue to her, goes mad. Lord Walter is excused by the Parliament for allowing the escape of his prisoner, but a large reward is offered for Lord Arthur ; nevertheless, he gains an interview with his love, Elvira ; she recognizes him, and in her frenzy, being anxious he should not again escape her, she

* Composed for Grisi, Rubini, Tamburini, and Lablache, and produced at the Théâtre des Italiens, Paris, Jan. 25th, 1835 ; in London, at the King's Theatre, May 21st, 1835.

·calls for help and he is seized by the guard. She then recovers her senses to find him a doomed prisoner. They are about to lead him off, when a messenger arrives bearing a despatch from the Parliament, which contains a free pardon to all political offenders, Cromwell having finally crushed the Stuart cause, and feeling that only by showing mercy could he gain future peace.

LA SONNAMBULA.*

THE scene of this opera is in Switzerland. For some time the villagers have been frightened by the appearance after nightfall of a figure in white at the village mill, all asserting it to be a ghost, whereas in reality it is Amina, daughter of Teresa, a peasant, and betrothed to Elvino, a young farmer. She is a somnambulist. All is arranged for the wedding to take place on the following morning, much to the discomfort of Lisa, the hostess of the village inn, who was formerly affianced to Elvino. In the midst of the festivities appears Rodolph, lord of the district, who is travelling home incognito after many years of absence, having been kidnapped away when a child. As night is fast closing in, he takes a bed at the village hostelry.

The second Act opens with Rodolph in his bedroom, when Lisa enters and tells him the villagers are coming to welcome him home. He makes rather pressing love to her, when they are disturbed by the sudden appearance of Amina walking in her sleep, who comes in through the window. Lisa hurries to hide herself in a closet, but in doing so drops her shawl. Amina in her sleep talks about her love for Elvino, and finally lies down on the Count's bed, who, picking up Lisa's shawl, wraps it about her, and then leaves by the window. The villagers, headed by Alessio, a peasant, enter the room, and all are taken aback on discovering Amina asleep on the Count's bed, and Elvino, seeing his affianced in such a position, vows he will not marry her.

In the next scene Amina and her mother, Teresa, are making their

---

* "La Sonnambula" was written at Milan in the year 1831 for Mme. Pasta, and was first heard in London in July of the same year. Pasta was born in 1798 at Como, near Milan; she was of Jewish extraction. During the latter years of her life she lived in retirement on Lake Como, and died April 1st, 1865.

Adelina Maria Clorinda Patti, one of the daughters of Salvatori Patti, made her *début* at Covent Garden Theatre in the character of Amina, May 14th, 1861. She was born at Madrid, April 9th, 1843, and first appeared on the stage in New York, Nov. 24th, 1859.

A no less remarkable singer made her *début* in the same character, in the person of Mme. Albani, at Covent Garden Theatre, on April 2nd, 1872. She is by birth a Canadian, and was trained by Duprez, the once famous tenor, at the Conservatoire.

way to the castle to ask the Count to tell the truth about the unfortunate adventure, and so to clear Amina's character, when they meet Elvino. Amina pleads her cause to him, but he is obdurate.

The final Act opens with Elvino about to lead Lisa, his old love, to the altar, when the Count arrives and declares Amina's innocence. Elvino will not believe it, but Teresa produces Lisa's shawl which was found wrapped about Amina in the Count's room. Elvino then demands an explanation from the Count, who says about Lisa he would rather say nothing, but protests that Amina is innocent. Elvino asks who shall prove it, when Amina appears again walking in her sleep along a plank above the water-wheel; she comes down among the astonished villagers, and talks in her sleep in such affectionate terms of Elvino that he is at length convinced of her innocence, and she wakes up to find herself in his arms.

BIZET.

GEORGES BIZET was born at Paris, Oct. 25th, 1838. During his but too short career (for he died June 3rd, 1875) he wrote the following operas:—"Docteur Miracle," produced at the Bouffes Parisiens in April, 1857; "Vasco di Gama," produced at the Théâtre Lyrique, Paris, in 1863; "Les Pêcheurs de Perles," produced at the Opéra Comique, Paris, Sept. 30th, 1863; "Djamileh," and his best work, "Carmen" (*vide* note). In the year 1857 he obtained in the Conservatoire, Paris, the Grand Prix de Rome.

CARMEN.*

CARMEN, the heroine of this opera, is a gipsy, and one of a band of smugglers; she is employed, with many other girls, in a cigarette factory in Seville. The most remarkable feature in her character is her coquetry and utter incapability of remaining true to one love for any length of time. The hero, José, a sergeant of dragoons, on the other hand, is of a passionate, jealous, and revengeful nature.

The opening scene is a square in Seville, in which the cigarette factory where Carmen is employed is situated. A crowd of people and soldiers are discovered singing. Micaela enters, a simple village maiden to whom José was affianced before he joined the army. She has come in search of him, to deliver a message from his old widowed mother. Not finding him, and being impertinently treated by Morales, an officer of dragoons, she runs away frightened. On José's entrance Morales acquaints him with the visit of Micaela. The mid-day bell then sounds, and the girls come pouring out of the factory, among them Carmen. The crowd of men ask her to select a lover, and she throws a flower at José, and runs off, followed by her companions. He is much struck with her beauty, and is cogitating over the adventure, when Micaela re-enters, who delivers the message from his mother, and he is so overcome by home recollections that he determines to think no more of Carmen. At

---

* Carmen was first performed in Paris on March 3rd, 1875; and in London at Her Majesty's on June 22nd, 1878, Mlle. Minnie Hauk taking the part of Carmen. An English adaptation of it was produced by Carl Rosa, at Her Majesty's, on Feb. 5th, 1879, Mme. Selina Dolaro sustaining the *rôle* of the heroine. The libretto is founded upon Mérimée's famous novel.

this moment a great noise is heard in the factory, and all rush out, declaring that Carmen has stabbed one of her companions. Zuniga, captain of dragoons, orders José to bind her and lead her off to prison. They are left alone for a few minutes while Zuniga writes out the order for her imprisonment, and Carmen makes good use of the time, for she succeeds in so working upon José's feelings that he, declaring his love for her, allows her on the way to the prison to escape.

The next Act is in the tavern of Lillas Pastia, outside Seville, a rendezvous of the smugglers. Carmen is discovered surrounded by gipsies and officers of dragoons, and Zuniga is paying his addresses to her, but without much success. He tells her how José has been imprisoned for a month for having allowed her to escape, but that he is to be set at liberty that night. Escamillo, the renowned toreador, or bull-fighter, happening to pass, they call him in. He is much struck with the beauty of Carmen, but she refuses all overtures, declaring she loves another. He says he will wait. Lillas Pastia clears the tavern of his guests, but Zuniga tells Carmen he will return an hour hence. When all have gone except Carmen and the other gipsy girls, two of the smugglers, Dancairo and Remendado, enter, who, with their companions, are making their way to Seville with a cargo of goods ; they ask the girls to join them and assist them in the work. Carmen declares she cannot until the morrow, as she is expecting her lover, José, and on his entrance they are left alone. She tries to persuade him to join the band, but he refuses, and is about to go back to the barracks, when the door is burst open by Zuniga, who, according to his promise, has returned. He orders his serjeant to retire, who, jealous, refuses. Zuniga draws his sword, on which José does the same, and they are about to cross blades, when Carmen rushes between them, calls for help, and the band of smugglers coming in, disarm and lead off Zuniga. José, seeing that all is over with his career in the army, joins the band.

The third Act is in a retreat of the smugglers, among the mountains. Carmen tells José she has lost her love for him on account of his jealousy, and begs him to leave her. He declares he will never do so until death parts them. The smugglers hurry off with their goods, leaving José alone as sentinel. Micaela enters, wishing to tell José of his mother, but, on hearing the report of a gun, she hides. Enter Escamillo, followed by José, who has fired upon but not injured him. He tells José he has come for Carmen, thinking it is about time she was sick of her soldier love. José, enraged, calls on him to defend himself, and they fight. Escamillo slips and falls, and José is about to plunge his knife into him, when the smugglers rush in and drag them apart. Escamillo then asks all to attend the bull-fight in Seville. The smugglers at this moment find Micaela and drag her out. She tells José his mother is dying; he, torn between jealousy and filial affection, at length gives way to the better feeling, but, on leaving, warns Carmen they will shortly meet again.

The last Act is a street outside the Plaza de Toros, showing the entrance to the circus. The crowd are assembled to witness the great bull-fight, and among them the gipsies. Carmen vows to Escamillo she has never loved any one as she loves him. All retire into the circus except Carmen and José, who has been hiding among the crowd. He begs her to fly with him, but she declares she loves him no longer. The crowd in the circus behind are heard singing in chorus the praises of Escamillo. Again and again does José plead his cause, but with no effect, and at last she throws the ring he had given her at his feet, and he, in a frenzy of jealousy, while the audience in the circus are still heard singing, stabs her to the heart. The crowd enter to find Carmen dead and José embracing her corpse.

CORNELIUS.

PETER CORNELIUS was born at Mayence, Dec. 24th, 1824. Destined originally for the stage, he soon abandoned that calling for music, studying, from 1845 to 1850, at Berlin, under Dehn. In 1852 he was at Weimar, where he joined the band of young musicians under the inspiring influence of Liszt. There it was that he composed "Der Barbier von Baghdad," where it was performed in 1858. Liszt was so disgusted at its bad reception, and the captious opposition that it met with, that in the following year he threw up his post of opera conductor, and went to live in Rome. Cornelius followed Wagner to Munich in 1865, and composed "Le Cid," and was working at a third opera, "Gunlöd," when death overtook him at Mayence, October, 1874.

DER BARBIER VON BAGHDAD.*

THE libretto is founded upon one of the tales in "The Arabian Nights." The scene of Act I. is a room in the house of Noureddeen, a wealthy young man of Bagdad. Noureddeen has fallen so violently in love with Morgana, the daughter of a Cadi of the city, that he is sick of a fever, and, as the curtain rises, is discovered lying upon a couch. Presently Bostana, a kinswoman of the Cadi, enters and tells him how he and Morgana can meet—that when the father goes to prayer at the mosque the daughter will be alone. She then arranges to send Aboul Hassan, a skilful barber, to make him neat and tidy for the meeting. Aboul Hassan presently enters, and in the ensuing duet Noureddeen is all impatience to be shaved, while the barber will not stop chattering about horoscopes, the stars, and boasting of all his wonderful learning. In despair Noureddeen calls in the servants to turn out the loquacious barber; but the latter draws out a razor, which he flourishes open, and drives the servants out. Noureddeen at length persuades Aboul to begin shaving him, and he tells him how he is going to meet Morgana. Aboul says he will accompany him. To prevent this Noureddeen calls in the servants once more, telling them that the barber is ill and needs attention. While they

* Produced at Weimar (one performance only) Dec. 16th, 1858, and revived at Munich, October, 1885. Given in English at the Savoy Theatre by the Royal College of Music, Dec. 9th, 1891.

surround and press unwelcome attentions upon the barber, Noureddeen escapes, and the curtain falls.

The second Act opens in the women's apartments of the Cadi's house. Morgana enters, and then Bostana, who tells her that Noureddeen is coming. At this moment the Cadi appears, and some servants bring in a chest containing gold and treasures from a certain Selim, who the Cadi explains is coming to woo Morgana. The call to prayers is heard without, and the Cadi goes off to the mosque. When he has gone, Bostana ushers in Noureddeen. The love duet is interrupted by the cries of a slave in another part of the house. Bostana enters hurriedly, says that the Cadi has returned, and is beating a boy who has broken a jar of olives. Then the voice of the barber is heard out in the street crying that some one is being murdered by the Cadi. As the disturbance increases Noureddeen is hidden for safety in the treasure-chest, just as the barber, accompanied by some of Noureddeen's servants, rush in. The barber asks where is his friend Noureddeen who is being killed. Bostana tells him he is in the chest; will he and the servants carry it out before the Cadi comes? As they lift it to do so, the Cadi enters and thinks that Aboul is robbing him. There is great commotion between the Cadi's servants and those accompanying the barber, which is stopped by the entrance of the Caliph demanding an explanation of the disturbance. Aboul says the box contains the body of his murdered friend; the Cadi says that what it contains belongs to Morgana. It is opened, and to the latter's great astonishment, there is disclosed the insensible Noureddeen. The Caliph understands there is a love affair, and on Noureddeen being revived, declares that as the Cadi said that the chest contained Morgana's property he must abide by the statement. In consequence the lovers are unexpectedly united, and the curtain falls on the Caliph's inviting all concerned to a wedding feast.

DONIZETTI.

GAETANO DONIZETTI was born at Bergamo on Nov. 25th (or 29th), 1797. His father had destined him for the profession of teaching, but he himself thought he had more taste for architecture. Both father and son were wrong, and nature asserting herself, soon showed what was the real bent of his mind. He studied music in the Lyceum at Bergamo, under Mayr, Salari, and Gonzales, and at Bologna, under Mattei and Pilotti. His first operatic work, entitled "Enrico Conte di Borgogna," was performed at Venice in the year 1818, and his last opera, "Catarina Cornaro," was written at Naples in the year 1844. On Aug. 17th, 1845, he had a stroke of paralysis, which affected his brain. All means were adopted to effect a cure, but without success, and, as a last resource, his friends determined to try what his native air would do for him. He was taken back to Bergamo, but died there on April 8th, 1848.

DON PASQUALE.*

NORINA, the heroine of this opera-bouffe, is a young widow, with whom Ernesto, a young Italian gentleman, is in love. Ernesto, of course, finds the course of love run anything but smoothly, owing to the prejudice of his rich uncle, Don Pasquale, who wishes him to marry some one else, and threatens to disinherit Ernesto if he does not comply with his wishes. But the lovers have a good friend in the family physician, Dr. Malatesta. Don Pasquale having consulted him with reference to his own marriage —the Don having determined to marry himself to spite his nephew—the doctor introduces Norina to him as his sister, suggesting that she would suit him.

The nuptials having been duly celebrated by a sham marriage ceremony, Norina plays her part in the plot against the Don by at once launching out into reckless extravagance—ordering carriages, horses, and new furniture, to the great chagrin of her mock husband. She also takes care to drop a letter in his way referring to an assignation with a

---

* Was composed at Paris in the year 1843, and there produced with the greatest success, no doubt partly owing to the admirable rendering of the Don by Lablache. Produced in London in the same year. Donizetti is said to have written out the score in eight days.

gallant in the garden. This is more than the old gentleman can bear. In a fury he repairs to Malatesta, and insists upon his coming to the garden with him to surprise his faithless wife. They find Norina there, and Don Pasquale orders her from the house, which she refuses to leave. In despair, he gives Malatesta *carte blanche* to do what he likes if only he can get rid of her. The Doctor tells him his only chance is to let Ernesto marry Norina, as then his sister will not stay in the same house with Norina. The Don consents, and is then told of the trick which has been played on him, and good-humouredly sanctions the marriage of Ernesto and Norina, glad to have escaped from what threatened to be a most unfortunate match for himself.

L'ELISIR D'AMORE.*

THE scene opens in the country. Reapers are resting beneath a tree, under which are seated also Adina and her friend Gianetta. Nemorino, a countryman, who is in love with Adina, stands near in a melancholy mood at the hopelessness of his suit, and overhears Gianetta reading a love-story to Adina, recounting how one Tristano succeeded in wooing his love, Isotta, by means of a love elixir given to him by a sage enchanter. Nemorino is fired with the determination to procure a similar love philtre to assist him in winning the love of Adina. In the nick of time Dr. Dulcamara, the notorious travelling quack doctor, arrives in the village to a sound of trumpets. Nemorino repairs to the doctor in his gilt chariot, who, for a piastre, supplies him with a bottle of what he wants. This in reality is but a bottle of wine. Nemorino drinks it, and it enables him so far to conquer his natural diffidence that he temporarily gets rid of his love-sickness, and succeeds in inducing Adina to think he does not care for her. She in womanly fashion is the more determined to hold him in her chains, and tortures poor Nemorino by promising to marry his rival, the sergeant Belcore, quartered in the village, who makes love in a far bolder fashion than the timid Nemorino. He is invited to the nuptials of the sergeant and Adina. He there meets Dulcamara, and asks for another bottle of the elixir. But he has no money. In despair, in order to procure the coin, he, by the sergeant's advice, enlists as a soldier, and so gets twenty crowns in his pocket. After the second dose he is convinced of its efficacy, for all the village

---

* Composed at Naples in the year 1832. Produced at Milan in the same year; and in London, at the Lyceum Theatre, Dec. 10th, 1836.

girls come round him, paying him a great deal of attention, the real cause of their changed behaviour being the fact that Nemorino's uncle has died and left him a fortune, of which he is at present unaware.

The dance is about to begin ; the girls are all importunate to secure Nemorino as their partner.   Adina is distracted, for she wishes to marry Nemorino now, while Dr. Dulcamara is perhaps the most astonished at the marvellous effects of his bottle, which he never anticipated.   He offers a bottle to Adina, but she knows better ; she has a better elixir in her own eyes wherewith to charm him, and she tells the Doctor so.   She pays the smart-money, and buys back from the sergeant Nemorino's contract for enlistment, meets her lover, and marries him.

In the last scene the discomfited sergeant has to salute his rival, and the disclosure is made that Nemorino has become a rich man owing to the death of his uncle.   Dulcamara vows he knew it all along, but there is something which the world does not yet know—the marvellous effects of his elixir, &c., &c., of which he there and then sells a number of bottles, re-mounts his gilt chariot, and passes on to the next town.

LA FAVORITE.*

THE scene is laid in Spain   Fernando, a novice, about to take monastic vows, suddenly startles his friends, the monks, by telling them that he is in love, and means to renounce the life of a priest, for which he was preparing himself.   The object of his admiration is one Leonora, who also loves him, but has not dared to disclose to him the fact that she is the " Favourite " for whom his Majesty Alphonso XI. is prepared to put aside his wife, and whom he then means to make the partner of his throne.   Fernando is the soul of honour, and Leonora, knowing this does not tell him who and what she is, but she procures for him a commission in the army from the King, and beseeches him never to see her again.   Meanwhile, the King is threatened with excommunication if he divorces his wife for Leonora, and shortly Fernando reappears, having greatly distinguished himself in war.   The King is ready to grant him anything.   He asks for Leonora's hand, not knowing who she is.   The King grants his request, and loads him with titles and honours.   The marriage is celebrated, when, to his horror, Fernando finds he has

----

* This opera, one of Donizetti's best productions, was performed at Paris in the year 1840. when it met with but a cold reception ; so much so, that the composer had difficulty in finding a purchaser of the score, and when he did so, only got 3.000 francs for it.   Produced in London, at Her Majesty's Theatre, Feb. 16th, 1847.   Jean de Reszke made his *début* at Venice in this Opera in January, 1874.

married the King's mistress. In a storm of indignation he renounces the King's service, breaks his sword, and leaves, to rejoin the monastic life he abandoned for Leonora's sake.

In the last Act Fernando is followed to the church, where he is preparing for his religious life, by Leonora. In a heart-breaking scene in church she tells him that she had always thought her confidante, Ines, had told him who she was, and implores his forgiveness. His love for her overcomes his scruples, so that he proposes to fly with her; but she refuses to put his soul in peril, and dies with the words of his love and forgiveness in her ears.

LA FIGLIA DEL REGGIMENTO.*

THE daughter of the regiment is Maria, a vivandière, attached to the 11th regiment of Napoleon's army, at this time invading the Tyrol. She had been found a child on the field of battle by Sulpizio, a sergeant of the regiment, and had been brought up, so to speak, as the child of the regiment. While in the French camp, a prisoner is brought in, a Tyrolese, Tonio by name, who on one occasion saved the life of Maria when she was on the point of falling over a precipice. She intercedes for him, and his life is spared, he consenting to join the regiment. It is scarcely necessary to say that they vow constancy to each other. Tonio obtains the consent of the regiment to his making Maria his wife, when the Marchioness of Berkenfeld appears in the camp, and to her Sulpizio hands a letter which was found on the body of the servant who had charge of Maria when she was first picked up, and which was addressed to the Marchioness. She claims Maria as her niece, who takes an affecting farewell of the regiment, leaving Tonio in distraction.

The second Act is laid at the castle of the Marchioness. She in vain attempts to teach Maria a love-song in the classical style, for her niece keeps breaking in with snatches of the regimental songs, in which she is encouraged by Sulpizio, who is at the castle with a wounded arm. Maria is bewailing her fate at having to marry a duke, whom her aunt wishes to be her husband, when the gallant 11th seize the castle, Tonio at their head, with the avowed determination to prevent the daughter of the regiment from being forced to marry against her will. Eventually the Marchioness allows her better feelings to get the upper hand, and, refusing to be the author of misery to Maria, who is in reality her daughter, and not her niece, she consents to her union with Tonio.

---

* Was first produced at the Opéra Comique, Paris, 1840.

LUCIA DI LAMMERMOOR.*

THE opera is founded on the story of Scott's "The Bride of Lammermoor." The scene is in Scotland in the last century. Henry Ashton, the brother of Lucy, wishes her to marry Arthur, whose aid he needs to support him in his feud with Edgar, the master of Ravenswood. Lucy and Edgar are in love with each other; they meet in secret and exchange mutual vows, previous to Edgar's leaving the country for France. Lucy refuses to marry Arthur, but is persuaded into doing so on being shown a forged letter—which her brother has had prepared—in which Edgar is described as faithless to her. She signs the marriage contract to save her brother, when Edgar suddenly appears. He is furious, and passionately returns her pledge of love, and seizes that which he had given her, trampling it under his feet.

In the last Act, at the bridal banquet, it is announced that a tragedy has taken place in the bridal bedchamber. Lucy is mad, and in her frenzy has stabbed her husband to the heart. Edgar is wandering among the tombs of his ancestors when the news is brought to him that Lucy is dying. He flies to see her once more, but is too late; and in his misery, and exclaiming that he will rejoin her, he plunges his dagger into his heart, and dies.

---

* Was composed and produced at Naples in the year 1835. Owing to the great success of the opera the composer was appointed professor of counterpoint to the Royal College of Music at Naples. Produced in London at Her Majesty's Theatre, April 5th, 1838. Mme. Melba made her first appearance at Covent Garden in this opera on May 24th, 1888.

GLUCK.

CHRISTOPH WILLIBALD RITTER VON GLUCK was born July 2nd, 1714. There is not space here to enter into a lengthy account of the important part played by this great composer in the history of opera. His influence in his own day was far reaching; sufficient now to observe that the beauties of his music remain as fresh as ever and marked by an atmosphere of classic grace and charm unapproached by any other writer for the stage. He showed a taste for music in his earliest years; in 1732 he was studying at Prague, and four years later was in Vienna. His early operas were produced in Italian towns with such success that he was invited in 1745 to London as composer to the Haymarket Opera. He returned to Vienna in 1755, producing in 1762 "Orfeo ed Euridice," the first of his great works. In 1776 "Alceste" was performed in Paris, followed by "Iphigenie en Aulide" in 1774, "Armide" in 1777, and "Iphigenie en Tauride" in 1778. At the height of his fame and in possession of a large fortune Gluck died at Vienna of an apoplectic stroke, Nov. 15th, 1787.

ARMIDE.

ARMIDE is the princess deeply versed in magic arts of the legend immortalized by Tasso. In the first Act, the scene of which is the palace of her uncle Hidraot, King of Damascus, she is lamenting to her attendants, Phœnicia and Sidonia, that the bravest knight in the army of the Crusaders, Renaud, or Rinaldo, has proved blind to her charms. Her uncle enters, entreating her to choose a husband; she answers she will marry none but the conqueror of the invincible Rinaldo. A chorus in praise of her charms ensues, and then there enters Aronte, a Paynim knight, who has been wounded in fruitless defence of his captives against a single knight. Armide says, "It is Rinaldo"; Aronte replies, "Yes, Rinaldo," and dies. The Act ends with vows of vengeance against this hero. The second Act opens with Rinaldo and Artemidor, a follower. The latter warns Rinaldo against the wiles of Armide. Rinaldo replies he scorns the spell of love and fears no magic. They retire as Armide and Hidraot appear, invoking the spirits of Rage and Hate. Rinaldo is seen approaching the bank of a stream, and Armide and the king withdraw. Rinaldo, attracted by the fairness of the scene, presently falls asleep. Spirits appearing as nymphs, shepherds, and shepherdesses enchant him during his slumber, spreading garlands round him. Armide now appears with a dagger, but love for the hero is awakened in her, and she cannot kill him, bidding instead the spirits of the air to bear them both away. In the first scene of the third Act Armide discloses the fact that Rinaldo rejects her love ; Phœnicia and Sidonia cannot console her, and presently she calls up the spirit of Hate. Hate and his satellites appear, but she finds herself unable to accept his aid ; love, after all, rules her too strongly. The fourth Act is concerned with the adventures of Ubalde and the Danish knight ; they are seeking for Rinaldo to rescue him from Armide. Two spirits, in the shape of Lucinda and Melissa, appear ; the first attracts the Danish knight, but is made to vanish by Ubalde, who touches her with a golden sceptre, while the knight rescues Ubalde in similar fashion from the attractions of the second. Act V. opens with a love duet between Armide and Rinaldo, for Rinaldo has at length succumbed to the charms of the princess. After a chorus and dancing, Rinaldo is left alone, and to him enter Ubalde and the Danish knight, who persuade him to forsake the slavery of love and return to his former life of victorious exploits. Rinaldo has a scene with Armide, who swoons as he tears himself away ; and the opera ends with her calling upon the demons to destroy the palace, while she is borne away in a winged chariot.

ORFEO ED EURIDICE.*

THIS famous story was the subject of the earliest operas ever written, those of Caccini and Peri and Monteverde, at the beginning of the seventeenth century. Gluck's version begins with the adorning of the tomb of Eurydice, while Orpheus stands by in profound grief. He calls upon the shade of his lost wife. Eros enters and tells him of the conditions imposed on him should he attempt to rescue her. In the second Act Orpheus at length succeeds in persuading the Furies to grant him passage to the Elysian Fields, to which the scene changes. Here Orpheus comes, charmed at the magical beauty, and presently he has to find Eurydice by touch and instinct, according to the conditions that were imposed. In the third Act Eurydice is grieved that Orpheus does not look at her ; but when he turns to do so, giving way to her reproaches, she sinks back lifeless. This is where the well-known " Che farò senza Euridice " is sung by Orpheus. Eros now appears again to say that the gods have had pity upon him and his grief, and transports him to the Temple of Love. His wife is restored to him, and so ends the opera with rejoicing.

---

* First heard in London at Covent Garden, June 27th, 1860.

GOUNOD.

CHARLES FRANÇOIS GOUNOD was born in Paris on June 17th, 1818. He received his musical education from Halévy (at the Conservatoire), Lesueur, and Paër. In the year 1837 he gained the second prize at the Institute, and in 1839 he carried off the first prize for his cantata entitled "Fernand." He was elected a member of the French Institute, Section of Music, in May, 1856, and was made Grand Officer of the Legion of Honour on July 6th, 1880. He died at St. Cloud, Oct. 18th, 1893.

The following is a list of Gounod's operatic productions :—"Sapho" —performed in Paris on April 16th, 1851 ; " La Nonne Sanglante "—produced on Oct. 18th, 1854 ; a comic opera, entitled " Le Médicin malgré lui"—first performed at the Théâtre Lyrique in Paris, 1858 ; "Faust " (*vide* note) ; "Philémon et Baucis "—produced at the Théâtre Lyrique on Feb. 18th, 1860 ; "La Reine de Saba," 1862—has been occasionally given in London under the name of " Irene " ; " Mireille," 1864—produced in London the same year ; "La Colombe," 1866 ; " Romeo and Juliet "— produced both in London and Paris in 1867 ; "Cinq Mars," 1877 ; " Polyeucte," 1878 ; and " Le Tribut de Zamora," 1881. His posthumous works include two operas, " Maître Pierre " and " Georges Dandin."

FAUST.*

FAUST, an old German student, or philosopher, having spent all his days in deep research into the secrets of nature, becomes disgusted with the smallness of his knowledge, and invoking the evil one, Mefistofele (*Mephistopheles*) appears. Faust begs him to restore to him his youth ; this the demon promises, on condition that Faust will sign a document. On his not much caring to do this, Mefistofele causes a vision to appear of a beautiful girl spinning, whom he promises to give to Faust. He at once signs, and, draining a goblet, is changed from an old, worn-out man into a handsome youth.

Margherita (*Margaret*), the maiden whom Mefistofele caused to appear to Faust in the vision, is a humble, pure-minded girl, with no relations

---

* This opera was first performed in Paris on March 19th, 1859, and proved the greatest success ; in London at Her Majesty's Theatre, June 11th, 1863, and in English at the same theatre the following year.

save one brother, Valentino (*Valentine*) ; and he, on leaving for the war, places her under the care of a kindly but foolish old dame called Marta (*Martha*), and a mere boy called Siebel, who is in love with Margherita. Against this unprotected maiden Mefistofele brings all his power to bear, merely using Faust as his agent to secure the death of her soul. The demon makes love to the chaperone Marta, while Faust is left to use all his powers to ingratiate himself with Margherita. He at first is unsuccessful, and is himself so struck with her pureness that he is on the point of relinquishing the diabolical scheme, but Mefistofele stifles the cries of his conscience, and Margherita, again assailed, gives way.

Valentine, returning from the war, and finding his once pure sister shunned by all, challenges Faust, her seducer, but is killed in the encounter, through the assistance of the demon. Margherita, on the death of her brother, goes mad, and in her frenzy kills the child she has borne to Faust. For this she is cast into prison and doomed to the scaffold. Overcome with remorse, Faust, accompanied by Mefistofele, who never leaves him, gains access to her prison ; he begs her to fly with him, but she refuses, telling him that to Heaven alone she looks for assistance, and, praying God to forgive her, falls dead at their feet.

A chorus of celestial beings is heard singing pardon to the repentant sinner, and the prison walls opening, disclose Margherita's soul being borne aloft toward heaven. Faust falls on his knees and prays, while Mefistofele, struck by the avenging sword of the Archangel, falls prostrate on the ground.

MIREILLE.*

THE story of Mirella is taken from a Provençal poem called "Miréio," written by Mistral.

In the first Act of the opera the heroine, Mirella, is seen with a group of village girls singing a pastoral chorus under the shade of a mulberry plantation When the song is ended the girls ask Mirella as to the truth of her being in love with Vincenzo, a handsome youth, who is only a poor basket-maker by trade. Mirella frankly acknowledges her affection, on which Tavena, a reputed witch, warns her to be cautious in her avowals, lest her father, Raimondo (a rich farmer), should not approve of the union. Vincenzo comes in, and the Act closes with expressions of devotion between the lovers.

The second Act opens with a dance in the arena at Arles. Here

---

* Produced in Paris, March 19th, 1864; in London as "Mirella," in Italian, July 5th, 1864.

Mirella and Vincenzo meet, but are separated in the crowd. Tavena tells Mirella that a fierce herdsman, named Urias, has been to Raimondo to ask for her hand in marriage, and soon afterwards Urias approaches Mirella and declares his affection, which she rejects with scorn. He retires in anger to report her refusal to her father. Vincenzo's father, Ambrogio (attended by his son, and his daughter, Vincenzina), next calls upon Raimondo and asks that Vincenzo and Mirella may be united, but the former indignantly refuses to consent. Mirella, overhearing this, rushes in and declares she will marry no one else. Raimondo flies into a violent passion and tries to strike his daughter, but is restrained by her falling at his feet and imploring mercy for her dead mother's sake. The two fathers now upbraid each other, the lovers renew their vows, Urias utters threats of vengeance, Vincenzina pours forth expressions of sympathy, and the curtain falls.

A harvest home is being held, in Act III., at Raimondo's farm. Mirella appears in deep dejection, and is soon joined by Vincenzina, with the news that Urias has wounded Vincenzo in the head with an iron trident, but that the latter is being tenderly nursed by Tavena. Mirella at once determines to go on a pilgrimage to the church of S. Marie, in the desert of Cro, in order to offer prayers for her lover's recovery. She is next seen in the desert struggling across the hot plains under the burning rays of the sun. A shepherd boy, Andreluno, goes by, singing a song in praise of the joys of pastoral life. Mirella's brain is affected by a sunstroke, and she sees a vision of Jerusalem in her madness, and pursues her way across the plain in hopes of reaching the holy city.

In the last Act she arrives at the church of S. Marie. A procession of pilgrims come in chanting psalms. Vincenzo is amongst the crowd and speaks to Mirella, but she does not know him at first. Eventually the sound of the sacred music restores her reason, and she falls into her lover's arms. Raimondo approaches and asks her forgiveness for his cruelty, Vincenzina and the pilgrims surround the group, and all join in singing a chorus of gratitude for the recovery and happiness of the faithful lovers.

ROMEO AND JULIET.*

In this opera Shakespeare's tragedy is very closely followed. The first Act opens in a hall in the house of Capulet, the father of Juliet, where a grand entertainment is being held. The chorus sing of the charms of dancing, &c. On the entrance of Juliet with her father, Paris,

---

* This opera was produced both in London and Paris in the year 1867.

to whom she is affianced, leads her off to the dancing saloon, and the rest follow. On their departure, Romeo, Mercutio, Benvolo, and others enter masked; they linger talking and laughing at Romeo about his ladylove Rosaline, when he, looking off, sees Juliet in the dancing room, and is so struck with her beauty that he at once falls desperately in love with her. They leave the hall, and Juliet enters with her nurse Gertrude; meantime Romeo re-enters with Gregory, an old servant of Capulet, and the latter by calling away the nurse leaves Juliet unintentionally alone with her new admirer. Romeo is declaring his love for her, when they are interrupted by the entrance of Theobald, her cousin, who, seeing through Romeo's disguise, recognizes him as a Montague, i.e., one of a race at enmity with the Capulets; he is about to insult him, but is stopped by Capulet, and Romeo is dragged away by his friend Mercutio.

The next Act is the well-known balcony scene. In this the librettist introduces a character unknown to Shakespeare, in the person of Stephano, Romeo's page. He is discovered helping his master by means of a rope ladder; he then leaves, taking the ladder with him. Romeo and Juliet are disturbed in their interview by the entrance of Gregory with servants and Juliet's old nurse, whose equilibrium has been disturbed by having found Stephano hanging about. They search the garden, but fail in finding any trace of Romeo, who, meantime, has hid. Juliet then joins them, coming from the house, which she re-enters with her nurse, but on Romeo again appearing, the servants having gone, she comes out, and they arrange to be secretly married on the following day in spite of her being betrothed to Paris.

The third Act opens in the cell of Friar Lawrence, who is discovered kneeling before a crucifix. Romeo enters, followed shortly afterwards by Juliet and her nurse, and on their demanding it, he then and there marries them, hoping thereby to end the feud between the two houses of Montague and Capulet. The scene then changes to a street in Verona, in which is situated Capulet's house. Stephano is discovered loitering about looking for his master; he then sings a song in the hopes of attracting the attention of the servants, and so hearing from them something of Romeo. They all flock out, headed by Gregory, who, on recognizing the page whom they had the night before driven away, is very wroth, and, after a little parleying, they cross swords. Enter Mercutio, Benvolo, Theobald and Paris, and lastly Romeo; the fight then becomes general. Theobald calls upon Romeo to fight with him, but he refuses, on which Mercutio takes up the matter and is mortally wounded. Romeo then draws on Theobald, and avenges the death of his friend by slaying him in his turn. Capulet and citizens then enter, attracted by the noise, and on seeing Theobald dying, vow vengeance upon Romeo, who declares himself ready to die. The Duke of Verona entering, all call on him to

avenge their wrong.   He tells Romeo to quit the country by daybreak—
who leaves, vowing to see Juliet once more.

In the fourth Act we are conveyed to the chamber of Juliet. She is
discovered with her husband, Romeo, sitting at her feet.   They talk of
the late tumult, and the death of her cousin, and of the hardship of their
lot, having thus to separate so soon after their marriage, &c. As day
breaks Romeo takes his departure, leaving by the balcony. Gertrude
then enters hastily to warn Juliet of the approach of her father, accompanied by Friar Lawrence. They enter, and her father then tells her
that she must marry Paris on the morrow. She is about to declare
herself the wife of another, but is stopped by the Friar and nurse.
Capulet and Gertrude then depart, leaving Juliet and Friar Lawrence
alone.   She vows she will sooner take her own life than undergo the
mock ceremony with Paris, but the Friar comforts her by giving her a
phial containing a potion that will cause her to sleep a sleep like death
for forty-two hours, and promises that after her funeral he will bring
Romeo to the tomb, when they can fly together. She takes it. Paris,
Capulet, and friends then enter, bringing the wedding ring. Juliet gradually swoons away, and falls at last apparently dead into the arms of her
father.

Act V. shows the interior of the tomb of the Capulets ; and Juliet,
apparently dead, is discovered lying in state. A noise is heard as of a
door being burst open, and Romeo enters. He is ignorant of the fact
of her having taken the potion, and imagines that he sees her corpse.
Overcome with grief, he takes a phial of poison from his pouch, and, pledg-
ing her in it, drains it to the last drop. Hardly is this done than Juliet
recovers from her trance. They are about to fly together, when he is seized
with faintness and tells her he has taken poison ; on his falling, she seizes
the phial, but, on finding it empty, draws a dagger, stabs herself, and
dies in the arms of her lover.

HUMPERDINCK.

ENGELBERT HUMPERDINCK was born at Siegburg (Rhine Provinces), Sept. 1st, 1854. He studied music at Cologne and Munich, and for some time lived in Italy, teaching theory at the Bologna Conservatoire. From 1890 to 1896 he was professor of harmony at the Hoch Conservatoire at Frankfort. During this time, in 1893 in fact, his world-famous "Hänsel und Gretel" was produced; it arrived in London in December of the following year. This opera was followed by another, "Der Königskinder," also given in London, which was scarcely so successful, although containing some fine music. A musical appointment was undertaken by him in Berlin in 1900, and he was made a member of the Senate of the Royal "Akademie der Künste." Later operas of his are "Dornröschen" (1902) and "Die Heirath wider Willen" (1905).

HÄNSEL UND GRETEL.

THIS charming work opens as follows: As the curtain rises, the two children, Hänsel and Gretel, are discovered in the poorly furnished room of a broom-maker's cottage, the boy making brooms, the girl knitting. They soon break away from their tasks and begin a romping dance. The mother enters and rates them for their laziness, finally packing them off into the wood to pick strawberries. In her anger, it may be noted, she upsets a jug of milk intended for their supper. She is crying at the poverty of the home, when the father's voice is heard in the distance, singing a rollicking song. He appears in high spirits, having sold a number of brooms and brought back plenty of food. The mother sets to work with her cooking, when she says she has sent the children into the forest. The father is horrified, and says that there lives the witch who lures children with magic gingerbread, only to pop them into the oven and serve them up for dinner. The curtain falls on the parents hurrying out of the house after the children. The scene of the second Act is laid in the forest. The children are gathering strawberries and making flower-garlands. Presently, as it gets dark, they realize they have lost their way, and are frightened. Mists rise in the background, and soon the Sandman, the sleep fairy, appears and throws sand in the children's eyes. They sing an evening hymn, and fall asleep. The mists lighten, and a stairway appears, down which angels pass, taking their places round the sleeping children, and forming a picturesque tableau as the curtain falls. Act III. opens with the same scene. The Dewman, or dawn fairy, enters and wakes the sleeping children. The mists still overhang the background, but as they clear away there is revealed, no longer the fir-trees, but the witch's house, made of sweetmeats. There is a fence in front of the house made of gingerbread figures. On one side is an oven, on the other a large cage. The children are enraptured at the sight, and presently make up their minds to go right up to the house and break off bits of cake from the walls. Unobserved, the witch appears and slips a noose round Hänsel's neck. Her attempts to catch the children, however, are eventually frustrated, as when the witch opens the oven door the children push her into it. There is an immense conflagration, the oven falls to pieces, and the next moment a troop of delighted children, freed from the enchantment, appears in place of the fence of gingerbread figures. All ends happily with the entrance of the father and mother.

LEONCAVALLO.

RUGGIERO LEONCAVALLO was born at Naples, March 8th, 1858. He studied music in the conservatoire of that town, and at an early age set to work on his first opera, the subject of which was the tragic story of Chatterton, the poet. But it was not until the production of "Pagliacci" that he achieved any success as an opera composer; since then he has composed several operas, one of which, " Der Roland," was a commission from the German Emperor, and was duly performed at Berlin in 1904. None of them seems likely to have the vogue of the earlier one, in spite of the undeniable cleverness and effective treatment of the dramatic situations.

PAGLIACCI.*

THE subject of this opera is said to have been founded upon fact, and the libretto was written by the composer himself. Before Act I. begins, Tonio, a strolling player, in his costume of clown, comes before the curtain and delivers the prologue, in which he says that the players have human hearts and human passions beneath the motley and tinsel of their trade. The curtain rises disclosing the wayside close to a village; a travelling theatre is on one side of the stage ; it is afternoon. Villagers enter, and presently the strolling players; Beppe, dressed as a harlequin, leading a donkey drawing a cart, in which Nedda, the columbine of the troupe, is lying, and Canio, her husband, in Punchinello costume. The last named invites the villagers to their performance in the theatre that evening. Nedda is now left alone ; she sings of the happy fate-led song-birds—who knows what they seek, whither they go? To her enters Tonio; he declares his passion for her; she rejects his advances, and has to defend herself with the donkey's whip, which Beppe had dropped on the stage. Tonio goes off, vowing vengeance. Silvio, one of the villagers, appears; he emplores Nedda to fly with him and leave for ever her husband, for whom she feels no love. As she consents, Canio, directed by Tonio, comes in, and, overhearing, rushes after the disappearing Silvio, while Tonio tells Nedda it is he who has betrayed her to her husband. Canio returns, and demands from Nedda the name of her

---

* Produced at Milan, May 21st, 1892 ; at Covent Garden, May 19th, 1893.

lover. She refuses to say, and Beppe, who comes in at that moment, is only just in time to prevent Canio from stabbing her with a dagger. The curtain falls on Canio alone, saying that no matter what one's feelings may be, the play must be acted ; the people pay, for them must the laugh be raised.

The scene is unchanged for the second Act. Beppe places benches in front of the theatre for the women of the audience just arriving for the evening performance. Silvio takes his place in front; as he pays Nedda (dressed as Columbine) for his seat, he says he will not fail to come for her that night. The players have all now entered the theatre ; its curtain rises, and the little play begins. The scene is a room with tables and chairs, &c. Columbine (Nedda) is awaiting her lover Harlequin (Beppe), as her husband Punchinello (Canio) is away. Taddeo (Tonio) enters from marketing, and makes exaggerated love to her. Harlequin comes and turns him out. Columbine and Harlequin sit down at the table to their meal. Taddeo enters to say that Punchinello is returning, and Harlequin makes a hurried exit. Punchinello now arrives, and asks who has been with her, half acting, half in earnest, as their situation in the play is similar to that of their real life. Finally, in a mad fit of jealousy, he stabs her. Nedda cries out, " Help me, Silvio ! " and dies. On hearing Silvio's voice, Canio turns upon him and stabs him. He is seized by the audience, and stands petrified as the curtain falls. [With acknowledgments to Messrs. Ascherberg, Hopwood & Crew.]

MASCAGNI.

Pietro Mascagni was born at Leghorn, Dec. 7th, 1863. His father, a baker, was at first strongly against the boy pursuing music. Eventually, however, his education, at the Institute Luigi Cherubini, was allowed to be continued. Here he studied for some time under Ponchielli and Saladino. Finding theory irksome, young Mascagni left and toured for some years with an opera company. Suddenly he became famous by winning the prize for an opera offered by Sonzogno, the publisher. This was " Cavalleria Rusticana," which has had an immense popularity, Other operas written later have been, in comparison, failures, " L'Amico Fritz " (1891), for example, or " Zanetta " (1896), and " Iris " (1898). " Le Maschere " was produced simultaneously (1901) in seven different cities, but at no theatre did it meet with great approval. " Cavalleria Rusticana " seems to be his *chef d'œuvre.*

CAVALLERIA RUSTICANA.*

The libretto of this opera is founded upon a well-known story of Sicilian village life of Giovanni Verga, by Signori Menasci and Targioni-Tozzetti. Before the curtain rises, Turiddu, a young peasant, sings, by way of prelude, a song of love to Lola, the wife of Alfio, a carter. When the stage is disclosed to view a village square is seen—a church on one side, an inn on the other. It is Easter, and the villagers enter singing, to keep the festival. Santuzza (who is betrothed to Turiddu) enters ; she asks Lucia, Turiddu's mother, where her son is. She is anxious as to his movements, suspecting his infidelity. Alfio comes in and sings a jovial song and of his faith in his wife Lola. From the church are heard the sounds of the Mass, and the chorus sing the Easter anthem and pass into the building. Lucia and Santuzza are left. The latter says that Turiddu and Lola were once betrothed, but when he came back from the wars he found her married ; that he became betrothed to her, but that now he has gone back to his old love. There now ensues a scene between Turiddu and Santuzza. She reproaches him for his faithless-

---

* Produced in Rome, May 18th, 1890, and in London, at the Shaftesbury Theatre, Oct. 19th, 1891.

ness, but he will not listen to her. Lola enters, singing a light and careless song; she goes into the church. Again Santuzza pleads with Turiddu; he throws her from him and hurries after Lola. Alfio enters, and Santuzza tells him that Lola has been faithless. The villagers come out of the church; Turiddu sings a drinking song, and when he offers Alfio a drink, the latter refuses it. Then follows the challenge according to the local custom, Turiddu biting Alfio's ear. Alfio goes out to await Turiddu in a neighbouring garden. Turiddu takes farewell of his mother and rushes off. Confused sounds from without are heard, and presently the cry, "Turiddu is killed!" Santuzza and Lucia fall senseless as the curtain descends. [By permission of the publishers, Messrs. Ascherberg, Hopwood & Crew.]

MEYERBEER.

GIACOMO MEYERBEER was a son of a wealthy banker, born at Berlin, Sept. 5th, 1791. All the family seem to have been highly gifted. Wilhelm Beer, brother of the above Giacomo, was a well-known astronomer, and Michel Beer, another brother, showed great promise as a poet, but died young. Giacomo Beer, as he then was, at a very early age displayed signs of his musical genius; he was accustomed when but four years old to play popular airs on the piano, putting his own accompaniment. His first master in music was Lauska. While under his care a friend of the Beer family died and left his property to little Giacomo, on condition that he would add to his own name that of the testator, which was Meyer, and so Giacomo Beer became Giacomo Meyerbeer.

On Oct. 14th, 1800, he performed on the pianoforte at a concert in Berlin. He studied for some time under Weber, and on leaving him he was for two years under the care of Abbé Vogler, at Darmstadt. When seventeen years old the Grand Duke appointed him composer to the Court. His first operatic work was called "La Fille de Jephté," and was first performed at Munich, Meyerbeer being then eighteen years old. In 1818 he produced "Romilda e Constanza," at Padua; 1819, "Semiramide riconosciuta," which was written at Turin for the actress Caroline Bassi; 1819, "Emma di Resburgo," or "Emma von Leicester"; and on Nov. 14th, 1820, "Margherita d'Anjou" was produced at La Scala, Milan; March 12th, 1822, "L'Esule di Granata," at La Scala, Milan; Dec. 26th, 1824, "Crociato," performed at Venice with great success, Mme. Meric Lalande and Lablache taking the principal *rôles*; 1831, "Robert le Diable," and after "Les Huguenots" and "Le Prophète," "L'Etoile du Nord," 1854; "Dinorah," 1859; and "L'Africaine," 1864. Meyerbeer died at Paris, May 2nd, 1864.

LES HUGUENOTS.*

THE scene opens at Tourain—a room in the Castle of Count de Nevers. A number of noblemen and gentlemen are present feasting; amongst others Raoul de Nangis, the leader of the Huguenots. In the midst of the revelry Nevers is called out to see a veiled lady, in whom Raoul recognizes Valentina, whom he met casually before, but whose name he does not know. Valentina is the daughter of Count St. Bris, the leader of the Catholics; and Marguerite de Valois, betrothed to Henri Quatre, having ascertained that Valentina has induced Nevers, whom she does not love, to give her up—he having been betrothed to her—by a ruse gets Raoul to Court, and endeavours to arrange a marriage between him and Valentina, with a view of putting an end to the feud between the rival factions of Catholics and Huguenots. Her plan prospers until Raoul sees Valentina, and recognizes in her the veiled lady he saw at Nevers' castle. He refuses the match, considering her character to be compromised, whereas, in reality, she went there only for the purpose of putting an end to her betrothal to Nevers.

The second Act opens with a scene on the banks of the Seine—a chapel in the background. The blended sounds of Huguenot hymns, Catholic litanies, and the coarse revelry of the citizens introduce a scene in which Valentina overhears a plot by her father, St. Bris, to assassinate Raoul. By the assistance of Marcel, Raoul's characteristic friend and follower, she prevents her father's base design from being carried out. St. Bris and Raoul meet outside the chapel for mortal combat, when the friends of both appear in force, and there is about to be a broil, when Marguerita enters and stops the conflict. Valentina also appears. Marguerita explains to Raoul that to Valentina he owes his life, and that his suspicions of her conduct in Nevers' house were unfounded. To his mortification, it is too late to mend matters, for Nevers steps from a boat and leads Valentina off in the midst of an assemblage of his friends come to witness the nuptials.

The third Act describes a secret visit of Raoul to Valentina. Her friends come in; she conceals him, and he overhears the plot to carry out the massacre of the Huguenots on St. Bartholomew's Eve concocted. Nevers refuses to join his friends, who place him under supervision.

---

* Was first performed at Paris, Feb. 29th, 1836. Mme. Theresa Tietjens first appeared before an English audience in the *rôle* of Valentina. She was of Hungarian extraction, born at Hamburg, 1831, where she made her *début* when only fifteen years old. She died at her residence in Finchley New Road, London, Oct. 3rd, 1877, and was buried on the 8th in Kensal Green Cemetery.

After a scene of intense passion between Raoul and Valentina, the former, showing her through the window what is passing in the street below, leaps to join his friends the Huguenots, and die with them.

The last Act opens with a ball in the Tour de Nesle, which is interrupted by the tolling of the great bell of St. Germains, and the guests hurry out of the room. The scene changes; first, to a cemetery and church, wherein Raoul and Valentina witness the massacre of the Huguenot women at their prayers in the church ; next, to a street on the quays of Paris. Raoul is mortally wounded, and is supported by Valentina. The Catholics, headed by St. Bris, come upon them. The soldiers fire at his command, and in his haste and zeal St. Bris finds he has caused his daughter's death. The Queen passes on her way from a ball at the Louvre, and the curtain drops on an opera full of thrilling action and situation.

LE PROPHÈTE.*

THIS opera is based upon the history of John of Leyden, the Prophet of the Anabaptists, who laid Germany waste in the name of God. According to their fanatical creed, their mission was to establish a theocracy, a community of property, and something like a community of wives. John of Leyden declared God had appeared to him and appointed him King, and his coronation was carried out with great pomp. Out of these historical facts the opera is, with some variation, constructed.

The scene is Holland. Fides, an old woman, keeps an inn near Dordrecht, and has a son John, the hero of the play. John is to marry Bertha, who is, however, a vassal of Count d'Oberthal, and has, therefore, to obtain his consent to her marriage. She goes with Fides to the Castle for that purpose; but Oberthal is smitten with her charms himself, and detains her. The Anabaptists, led by Zacharia, Jonas, and Mathison, protest and threaten, but the Count is inexorable. The three Anabaptists approach John with a view to enrolling him as their leader, and he half yields. Bertha escapes from her gaolers and flies to John, who conceals her ; but, on the Count's soldiers threatening his mother's life, he gives up Bertha, after a struggle with his feelings, and, half in religious ecstasy, half in desire for revenge upon Oberthal, becomes the Prophet of the Anabaptists.

The scene changes to their camp. Oberthal himself is brought in in the dark. He is sworn in as a member of the Anabaptist army—the tent being dark, and he thinking to aid his own escape by so doing—but a light is struck, and he is recognized. He is about to be killed, when John, hearing from him that Bertha is still alive, and in Munster, spares his life for the time being, and leads his army to the taking of the town.

Fides has no notion that it is her son who is the Prophet; she only knows that he has deserted her for the Anabaptists. She meets Bertha in the streets of Munster when the Anabaptists are in possession. In their ignorance they mutually denounce the Prophet who has robbed them of John, and vow vengeance. John is crowned in state, but his mother recognizes him in the street. She is disowned by him, and hurried to a dungeon. There Bertha appears, prepared to set fire to gunpowder in the vaults to destroy her enemies. John comes there to see his mother. Bertha recognizes him, and, finding he is the Prophet, renounces him for his deeds of massacre, and ends her life by stabbing herself in his presence. John is overcome with remorse, and determines to fire the vault pointed out by Bertha, and involve in common destruction the cruel Anabaptists, Oberthal, and his enemies, who he hears from an officer have by treachery gained admittance to the castle. He repairs to the coronation banquet. Oberthal, the bishop, nobles, and princes enter, but the gates close upon them. The walls fall in, the flames burst out, the mine is fired. Fides rushes in and dies with her son and his enemies and traitorous friends in the general ruin of the castle.

MOZART.

JOHANN CHRYSOSTOMUS WOLFGANG MOZART was son of Johann Leopold Mozart, Master of the Chapel at Salzburg, and grandson of a bookbinder at Augsburg. He was born at Salzburg, Jan. 27th, 1756. His mother was one Maria Anna Pertl. When but three years old Mozart would pick out on the harpsichord—the pianoforte of that day—musical intervals, such as thirds, sixths, &c.; and when he got them correct would show the greatest delight. At four years old he composed some minuets and other small pieces, which his father copied out. For three years his father travelled about the continent with him and his sister, Maria Anna Mozart, born Aug. 29th, 1751, giving musical entertainments; and everywhere the little Mozart won overwhelming applause for his astonishing performance on the harpsichord. In 1764 they visited England, and played before King George III., Mozart being then aged eight years.

In 1766 Mozart commenced studying composition under his father at Salzburg. His first dramatic production was a small opera, entitled "Bastien et Bastienne," which was written in the month of January, 1768. Mozart died Dec. 5th, 1791, aged under thirty-six years. He married, Aug. 4th, 1782, Constance Weber, a well-known pianist, and sister of Mme. Lange, the celebrated singer. She married, secondly, a councillor of Nissen, and died at Salzburg, March 6th, 1842. Mozart had two sons, Charles, born 1784, and Wolfgang Amadeus, born July 26th, 1791, just three months before his father's death. The latter became a pianist of some note, and died July 30th, 1844.

DON GIOVANNI.*

THIS opera depicts the career of Don Giovanni, a licentious nobleman who had deserted his wife, Elvira, and given himself up to a life of pleasure. In all his adventures he is assisted by his servant, Leporello, who, nevertheless, is shocked with his master's conduct.

---

* "Don Giovanni" was produced at Prague, Oct. 29th, 1787, with the greatest success. At Vienna it was not quite so well received. It is related that Haydn, on being asked his opinion of this opera, said, "I am not capable of judging: all that I know is that Mozart is certainly the greatest composer now in existence." It was first heard in London at the King's Theatre on April 12th, 1817.

In the first Act, Don Giovanni, having first insulted Donna Anna, then kills in a duel her father, the commandant of Seville, and escapes unrecognized. Don Ottavio, the lover of Donna Anna, vows to be revenged upon the unknown assassin. His next adventure is in a garden. Overhearing a lady deplore the unfaithfulness of her lover, he advances to offer consolation, when he discovers her to be his neglected wife, Elvira, who, with scorn, orders him to leave her. This he does, telling his servant, Leporello, to explain matters to her, who, in the song, " Madamina, il catalogo," gives a long list of all her husband's *affaires de cœur.* Don Giovanni next becomes enamoured of a peasant girl called Zerlina, who is betrothed to Masetto; but while making love to her his wife suddenly appears upon the scene and warns the girl against him.

In the next scene Don Ottavio and Donna Anna beg Don Giovanni to assist them in tracking the assassin of the commandant. He is promising to help them, when his wife enters and lays bare his dissolute life to them. Donna Anna then, for the first time, suspects him of being the insulter of herself and the murderer of her father. Don Giovanni next gives a large ball which Don Ottavio, Donna Anna, and Donna Elvira attend, masked. During one of the dances Don Giovanni succeeds in enticing Zerlina to enter a neighbouring apartment with him, but her screams for help attracting the dancers, they burst open the door, and Donna Elvira, unmasking, again exposes his conduct to all his guests. With this scene ends Act I.

In the second Act, Don Giovanni, being enamoured of his wife's maid, changes dresses with Leporello, thinking, thus equipped, the better to carry out the adventure. Masetto, meanwhile, having collected together a band of peasants, has determined to kill Don Giovanni; but he escapes, owing to his being mistaken for Leporello, and, by a ruse, succeeds in disarming Masetto, and in giving him a good beating. Leporello, on the other hand, is nearly killed by Don Ottavio, through being mistaken for Don Giovanni.

The next scene is in the cemetery, where is a statue to the memory of the late commandant. Don Giovanni and Leporello are arranging further adventures, when the statue speaks, warning Don Giovanni that his career must end with daybreak. He (Don Giovanni), nothing abashed, asks, in joke, the statue to sup with him; the invitation is accepted.

The last scene is the banqueting hall. Donna Elvira begs Don Giovanni to give up his wild life and return to her; he scoffs at the notion. She is leaving him broken-hearted when the statue appears, who, refusing to eat, invites Don Giovanni to sup with him. He accepts. The statue then seizes his hand, an icy chill passes through the frame of Don Giovanni, and he at length comprehends the awful doom in store for him. Here with the death of Don Giovanni and the disappearance of the statue the opera is generally brought to an end. There is a final scene, however, in which the other characters appear. Leporello explains what has happened, and a beautiful ensemble follows, in which the voices declare that thus is evil ever rewarded.

LE NOZZE DI FIGARO.*

THIS opera is founded upon Beaumarchais' comedy, "Les Folies d'un Jour." It is, so to speak, a collection of ridiculous *dénouements*, occasioned by the gallantries of the Count Almaviva and his household. The main feature of the opera is the intrigue between the Count and his wife's maid, Susanna, who is betrothed to Figaro, the Count's valet. Cherubino, the page, having been caught by his master closeted with Barbarina, comes to tell Susanna of his misfortune. The footsteps of the Count outside disturbs their interview, so Cherubino hides behind a large arm-chair. The Count then enters, and is explaining to Susanna how he has been made ambassador to the English Court, when Basilio, an attendant of the Count, is heard outside. Wishing to test what Basilio would say of him behind his back, the Count determines to hide. Susanna so manages matters that as the Count hides behind the chair Cherubino creeps round from the back and curls himself up in the chair; she then throws a dress over him. On Basilio telling Susanna that all the world knows that Cherubino is in love with his mistress, the Countess, the Count rises from behind the chair in a great rage and vows he will send the page away. Susanna pleads for him on account of his youth, but the Count will not hear of it, and then describes how he found the young rascal hid under the table in Barbarina's room. Suiting the action to the word, he lifts the dress from the chair, and to his astonishment again discloses the hiding Cherubino.

The final *dénouement* is caused by the Countess changing dresses with Susanna, and making an assignation with the Count in the garden. He is completely taken in; but, on seeing Figaro making love to the sham Countess, he is so incensed with jealousy that he calls for assistance, to expose his wife's infidelity, only to call the laugh of all against himself. He then becomes very repentant, and, on promising to turn over a new leaf, is forgiven by his wife.

There is also a sort of underplot running through the piece. Bartolo,

---

* "Le Nozze di Figaro" was written, by order of the Emperor Joseph II., in 1786. First performed on May 1st, the same year, at Vienna; in London at the King's Theatre, June 18th, 1812.

an old man, is determined to marry Susanna, who has already rejected
him, and Marcellina, an old woman, wishes to lead the unwilling Figaro to
the altar; but their plans fail on Marcellina finding that Figaro is her son
by a mark upon his arm, and declaring Bartolo to be his father.

IL SERAGLIO.*

THE Lady Constance and her maid Blonda having been taken prisoners,
are sold as slaves to the Bashaw Selim, who falls desperately in love with
Constance; but she in no way returns his affection, and makes a present
of Blonda to his factotum, Osmin. Meantime Belmont, son of Latades,
the Spanish Governor of Kan, and the affianced lover of Constance,
accompanied by Pedrillo, his servant, determine to effect the escape of
the Lady Constance and her maid. Belmont and Pedrillo manage, by
pretending to be the one an architect, the other a great gardener, to get
into the service of the Bashaw, and though trusted by him, they are hated
by Osmin, who is continually vowing vengeance upon them. They succeed in arranging with Constance and Blonda to be under the former's
window at midnight with a ladder, Belmont having a ship in the harbour
ready to carry them off. Pedrillo then makes Osmin, although a
Mahometan, very drunk, and puts him to bed; they are in the very act
of stealing away, when Osmin, now somewhat recovered from his unusual
libations, enters, calls the guard, and they are all taken prisoners and
brought before Selim. He threatens to have them tortured, but, finally
relenting, allows them to depart, much to the discomfort of Osmin,
who, after giving vent to his feelings—saying what he would do to
them were he Bashaw—makes his exit, raging.

DIE ZAUBERFLÖTE; OR, IL FLAUTO MAGICO.†

THIS opera deals with the mysterious worship of Isis, a goddess of
the ancient Egyptians. Tamino, an Egyptian prince, being chased by a
magic serpent, falls unconscious upon the ground. Three veiled ladies—
the attendants of Astrifiammante, the wicked Queen of the Night—kill
the serpent. They show Tamino the portrait of Pamina, daughter of the
Queen, whom Sarastro, High Priest of Isis, has carried away from her

---

* This opera was first performed in Vienna on July 16th, 1782; in England, in a
much distorted version, music cut out and replaced by other popular airs, at Covent
Garden, Nov. 24th, 1827.
† Was finished in July, 1791, and played for the first time on Sept. 30th following
at Vienna. Produced in London in Italian at the King's Theatre, June 6th, 1811.

mother to bring her up in the paths of virtue, and persuade Tamino, accompanied by Papageno, a talkative and untruthful bird-catcher, to undertake to return her to her mother. For this purpose they appoint three boys as attendants to guide them to the place where Pamina is held prisoner; to Tamino they give a golden flute, which, when played, will protect him from all dangers, and to Papageno another flute and bells for the same purpose.

Pamina has been placed by Sarastro under the care of Monostatos, a Moor, who is the head of his slaves. He is continually pressing his love upon Pamina, and because she does not return it he ill-uses her. Papageno manages to get an interview with her, and tells her of Tamino. She is about to run away with him, when she is stopped by Sarastro, to whom she confesses the truth, and tells him about Monostatos, whom he orders to receive seventy-seven stripes from the bastinado. On this occasion Pamina and Tamino meet for the first time, and Sarastro promises that they shall be united if they will undergo certain mysterious trials; and they are accordingly conveyed to the Temple of Isis.

The first test put upon Tamino is to be parted from his love, Pamina, and he is ordered to keep silence. The three veiled ladies appear to him and Papageno, and try to persuade them that Sarastro merely intends taking their lives. Papageno is much frightened, but Tamino remains true to his vows of silence. Monostatos, nothing daunted by his bastinadoing, attempts to kiss Pamina as she is sleeping in a garden, but is prevented by the sudden appearance of the Queen of the Night, who awakens her daughter, and tells her her only way of winning Tamino is to kill Sarastro, and seize on the gold symbol, and so leaves her. Pamina is horrified, when Monostatos comes in, who offers in return for her love to do the deed for her. On her refusing, he is about to stab her, but Sarastro, the priest, appears, who drives him from his service. Monostatos leaves, and joins the service of the Queen of the Night.

Tamino is again tested, by Pamina appearing to him and using the most affectionate terms, but he withstands the trial, and keeps silence. He is then led off to undergo further tests. Papageno wishes for a wife, and is promised, on certain conditions, one just like himself, whose name shall be Papagena. These conditions he fails in keeping, so an old woman appears to him, who makes violent love ; he promises to be a good husband to her, when she is suddenly transformed into Papagena. On this he rushes to embrace her, but the earth opens and he sinks into an abyss. Pamina, despairing of ever seeing Tamino again, attempts to take her own life with the dagger given her by her mother, but is prevented by the three boy-attendants on Tamino.

The next scene is a great mountain, at the foot of which is a cavern with a grating in front, from which issue flames. Tamino is told that if he dare pass through he will be able to devote himself to the mysteries of Isis. He and Pamina enter, they embrace, and, hand in hand, pass through the flames unscathed. The mountain changes to another, from which rushes a violent torrent, into which Tamino and Pamina enter, but are swept away from sight. The mountain opens, and they are discovered in a temple returning thanks. Papageno, has, to his great joy, Papagena returned to him.

In the last scene the Queen of the Night, attended by the three veiled ladies and Monostatos, rises from the earth. They are plotting the destruction of Sarastro, when, amidst the rolls of thunder, the scene changes to the Temple of the Sun. The Queen's sceptre having been broken, she and her attendants sink into the earth. Sarastro is seen seated on the throne, and Tamino and Pamina at the foot of it, attired in the habits of the initiated, are surrounded by a band of priests, who, in chorus, sing to the glory of their faithfulness through the trials imposed upon them.

NICOLAI.

CARL OTTO EHRENFRIED NICOLAI was born at Königsberg, June 9th, 1810. He studied music in Berlin under Zelter and Klein, and at Rome under Baini. For a short time he was capellmeister of the Kärnthner-thor Theater at Vienna. His first operas were produced in 1839 at Trieste, and met with success. In 1841 he was back at Vienna as first capellmeister of the Court Opera. He founded the Philharmonic Concerts in 1842, with the principal object of giving first-rate performances of Beethoven's symphonies. In 1844 he was made court capellmeister of the opera in Berlin, where the first performance of his "Die Lustigen Weiber von Windsor" took place on March 9th, 1849. But the composer did not live to enjoy its success, as he died on May 11th that same year.

DIE LUSTIGEN WEIBER VON WINDSOR.*

THE libretto is, of course, founded upon Shakespeare, and was written by Mosenthal. The framework of the play was altered, the order of events changed, and fresh incidents introduced, but otherwise the spirit of the original was well preserved. The opening scene of the first of the three Acts shows us a street in Windsor. Mrs. Ford comes out of her house reading the letter from Falstaff expressing his admiration. Mrs. Page appears with *her* letter couched in the same terms. The two go off planning how best to punish the knight. After some short dialogue between Ford, Page, Pistol, and others, there ensues a duet between Page and Fenton, in which the latter sues for the hand of Page's daughter Anne. Page says he intends her to marry Slender. The scene changes to a room in Ford's house. Mrs. Ford is alone, she is awaiting Falstaff's arrival, to whom she has sent a note. Mrs. Page enters and says she has written to Ford telling him to come in half an hour's time ; she goes off, and Falstaff enters. The duet between Mrs. Ford and Falstaff is inter-rupted by Mrs. Page knocking at the door. Falstaff hides behind a screen. The two wives frighten the knight by their pretended anxiety as to Ford's expected arrival. They persuade him to seek safety in the dirty-

---

* After the Berlin production, the opera was given in Vienna, 1852, and in London, as "Falstaff," on May 3rd, 1864, in Italian. The Carl Rosa Company brought out an English version at the Adelphi on Feb. 11th, 1878.

linen basket. The servants carry out the basket as Ford and a crowd of neighbours enter. Ford, of course, is wildly jealous, the house is searched, and the curtain falls on his asking his wife for her forgiveness.

The first scene of the second Act is the Garter Inn. Falstaff complains how he was thrown out of the basket into the river. Bardolph enters with a note from Mrs. Ford, to say that she wishes to make amends for his unfortunate experience, and invites him to come again that morning. A chorus of hunters enter, and Falstaff sings a drinking song. The chorus go out as Ford appears disguised as Brook. Falstaff promises to help him in the subjection of Mrs. Ford. The scene changes to a garden of Page's house. Slender enters, and sings of his affection for Anne ; as Caius appears, Slender hides. The doctor sings in the same strain, also hiding on Fenton's approach. After Fenton's love romance, Anne comes in, and the lovers have a duet; later. the other two from their hiding places joining in the finale ensemble. The scene changes again to the room in Ford's house. Falstaff and Mrs. Ford enter, but their conversation is interrupted by Mrs. Page. Falstaff goes into an inner room. Mrs. Page says that Ford is again on the alert, and has heard all about the escape in the basket. Falstaff enters, in alarm, and the women decide to dress him up as the old woman of Brentford. Ford now comes in ; he searches the basket, finding only linen inside ; and the curtain falls on Ford beating the disguised Falstaff out of the room.

The first scene of the third Act is the interior of Page's house. Mrs. Page, Mrs. Ford, and their husbands, plan how to punish Falstaff. Page and Mrs. Page in turn issue instructions to Anne how she is to be dressed, the one that Slender may recognize her and the other that Dr. Caius may do the same. Anne is left alone, and decides that the way out of the difficulty is to send dresses of the distinctive colours to Slender and Caius, so that they may each mistake the other for her. She then sings a song of her fidelity to Fenton. The final scene is that of Windsor Park. After a trio, in which Falstaff offers his heart to both Mrs. Ford and Mrs. Page, there ensues the fairy ballet and the rough and tumble treatment of Falstaff. The opera ends with a final clearing up, of the discomfiture of Caius and Slender, who had duly run off with each other, and the success of Anne's scheme to give herself to Fenton.

PONCHIELLI.

AMILCARE PONCHIELLI was born at Paderno Fasolaro, Cremona, on Sept. 1st, 1834. He studied music at the Milan Conservatoire, producing his first opera, "I Promessi Sposi," in 1856. Several other operas followed with increasing success, until the production in 1876 of what is, perhaps, his best known work, "La Gioconda." Later operas, "Il Figliuol prodigo" and "Marion Delorme," were brought out at Milan in 1880 and 1885. Ponchielli died in January of the year following this last production.

LA GIOCONDA.*

THE libretto of this opera is founded upon a play of Victor Hugo. The scene of the first Act is the courtyard of the Ducal Palace in Venice, the period being the seventeenth century. Holiday-makers fill the stage, presently going off to a regatta. Barnaba, the chief spy of the Council of Ten, is on the stage ; he observes Gioconda and her blind mother, La Cieca, approach. He is deeply enamoured of the former, and presently accosts her. She escapes from his grasp and goes out. It occurs to him he can influence her through her mother, and when the regatta folk come in he persuades the loser of the race, Zuane, that La Cieca, through witchcraft, has been the cause of his defeat. The populace seize upon the supposed witch. Enzo, a Genoese noble, but disguised as a mercantile captain, appears and protects her, calling on his comrades for help. At this moment Alvise, the chief of the Council of Ten, and Laura, his wife, enter. They set La Cieca free. Meanwhile Laura and Enzo recognize one another, having formerly been betrothed. Barnaba becomes aware of this, and realizes who Enzo really is. Laura accepts a rosary from La Cieca, and all go into the church, except Enzo and Barnaba. The latter taxes Enzo with his identity. Enzo replies he is a Dalmatian sailor betrothed to Gioconda. Barnaba says he knows who he is, that although he has pledged himself to Gioconda, he is really enamoured still of Laura, and, moreover, promises him that he, Barnaba, will arrange to bring her to Enzo's ship that night during her husband's absence at a meeting of the

---

* Produced at Milan, April 8th, 1876 ; at Covent Garden, May 31st, 1883 ; and in English at the Kennington Theatre, May 6th, 1903.

Council. Enzo departs, ready to give up Gioconda on the chance of once
more seeing Laura. Barnaba now dictates a letter to Alvise warning
him that his wife will elope with Enzo. Gioconda has appeared on the
scene ; unseen, she overhears this proof of her lover's perfidy. Her
lamentations are heard while the final chorus is sung by the people
in the church and the carnival revellers on the stage. The
scene of Act II. is part of a lagoon. Enzo's ship is visible ; there is a
chorus of sailors. Barnaba enters, disguised as a fisherman. He arranges
with his confidant, Isèpo, to have the war-galleys ready for the capture
of Enzo, and goes off. Enzo appears, sings his aria, "Heaven! and
Ocean!" and to him comes Laura. Their love duet over, Enzo descends
into the cabin, and Gioconda enters. Gioconda, in her jealous rage, is
ready to stab Laura, but sees a boat approaching, and tells her that it is
her husband. Laura, producing the rosary, utters a prayer. Gioconda
recognizes it as the one given to her by her mother, and determines to
save her, doing so by hurrying her into her own boat. Barnaba appears
to find Laura gone, and goes off in pursuit. There now follows a scene
between Enzo and Gioconda, who has re-entered. Enzo is obdurate to
Gioconda's entreaties, and, thinking all is now lost, when she tells him
he has been betrayed by Barnaba, sets fire to his ship as the curtain
falls. In the third Act Alvise determines to reward Laura's infidelity
with death, and prepares poison for her to take. Gioconda enters and
exchanges the poison for a sleeping draught, so that when Alvise returns
to find the empty phial on the table, and Laura lying in the adjoining
chamber, thinks her to be dead. The scene changes to a ball-room,
Alvise welcomes his guests ; there is a ballet, after which Barnaba
appears dragging in La Cieca, whom he had found in one of the reserved
apartments. She says she has only been praying for "her just dead."
The guests ask who. Enzo, who is in disguise, asks Barnaba who is
dead. He is told Laura. He thereupon unmasks and denounces Alvise.
Alvise throws back a curtain revealing the motionless body of Laura.
Enzo is seized by the guards, while Barnaba, in triumph, exacts a
promise from Gioconda to be his if he will save Enzo's life. The fourth
Act and last is situated on the edge of the Organo Canal. Laura,
enveloped in a cloak, is brought in to Gioconda. She is taken within, and
Gioconda resolves on suicide, and then is tempted to make away with
Laura, who is thus so safely within her power. But Enzo comes in. He
is furious when she tells him that she has removed Laura's body from
the tomb, and will not say where she is. He is about to stab her, when
Laura, within, wakes from her trance and calls out. She comes in, sees
Enzo, and they go out together. Barnaba now enters in time to prevent
Gioconda escaping, but to save herself from him she stabs herself and
falls dead.

PUCCINI.

GIACOMO PUCCINI was born at Lucca, June 22nd, 1858. He comes from a musical stock, many of his forbears having achieved no small reputation as composers of church music. Ponchielli was Puccini's principal teacher at the Milan Conservatoire. Early operas, such as " Le Ville " (1884), " Edgar" (1889), and, most of all, " Manon Lescaut " (1893), showed all the originality and promise that were matured in " La Bohème." This opera it was that proved Puccini to be without doubt an opera composer of genius, and since then each fresh work has been awaited with as much interest as the production has been successful.

LA BOHÈME.*

FOUNDED upon Henri Murger's novel, this libretto is constructed so as to show in four scenes some of the principal events, and to give a picture of Bohemian life in Paris. In the first Act we see the poverty-stricken Bohemians—Rodolphe the poet, Marcel the painter, Colline the philosopher—in a careless mood, notwithstanding the fact that the poet has to sacrifice his tragedy to keep the fire going. Enter Schaunard the musician, with provisions, the result of a dance engagement. Hilarity reigns, and the landlord, who calls for his rent, is made to drink deeply, and is finally turned out. Rodolphe is left to finish an article as the others go off to keep Christmas Eve at a café. Mimi, an embroideress, who lives on the same floor, now comes in, asking for a light as an excuse for so doing. There ensues a love-duet between the pair, after which they go off to join their friends. The scene of the second Act is a café, where we are introduced to a new character, Musette, with whom Marcel had once been in love. She enters with her new lover, Alcindoro, recognizes Marcel, and eventually sending Alcindoro off to buy her some new shoes, she joins the painter once more, and the friends go, leaving Alcindoro to pay for their supper. The scene of the third Act is the outside of a tavern adjoining a toll-gate. It is winter, and

---

* Produced at Turin, Feb. 1st, 1896 ; in England, in English, at Manchester, April 27th, 1897 ; and in Italian, at Covent Garden, July 1st, 1899.

early dawn. Mimi enters and explains to Marcel, who comes out of the inn, where he is living with Musette, that Rodolphe is so jealous that they are no longer happy together. Her violent fits of coughing are the signs of consumption. Marcel says he will speak to Rodolphe, and bids her hide herself behind some trees. The poet enters from the inn, and is overheard by Mimi telling Marcel that while he loves her still, he is madly jealous, and that, moreover, he suspects that she is ailing, growing weaker day by day. Mimi's cough and tears reveal her presence. She comes forward. Eventually they patch up their little quarrel. Meanwhile, Marcel, who had returned to the inn, comes out again with Musette, blaming her for flirting. They quarrel and separate, the curtain falling upon Rodolphe and Mimi going away together. In the final Act the scene is once more the attic of Act I. Marcel and Rodolphe are each endeavouring to forget their quarrels with their respective mistresses in their work, for neither couple have been together for some time. Schaunard and Colline enter with some provisions of a scanty nature. They get excited and begin dancing, when Musette suddenly comes in ; she has brought Mimi with her, Mimi who is now dying. She is brought into the room and laid on a bed. Rodolphe and Mimi are left alone as the others go off for a doctor and medicine. But it is too late, and the friends only return to a scene of grief, Rodolphe flinging himself in despair upon Mimi's lifeless form.

MADAMA BUTTERFLY.*

The libretto of this "Japanese tragedy" was written by Signori Illica and Giacosa, and was founded upon the book of John Luther Long and the drama of David Belasco. The locale is Japan, and the period the present day. The scene of Act I. is the exterior of a Japanese house, with terrace and garden overlooking the bay and harbour of Nagasaki. As the curtain rises, Goro, a marriage-broker, is showing Pinkerton, an American naval officer, over the house the latter has just bought, in which he is going to live with "Madame Butterfly," a Japanese girl with whom he is about to contract a "Japanese marriage." All is ready for the arrival of the bride, including the three servants whom Goro introduces—one of them is Suzuki, who is the Butterfly's handmaid—when Sharpless, the American Consul, enters. When Pinkerton explains what he intends doing, and that his "marriage" is one to bind him only as long as he

---

* First performed at La Scala, Milan, in 1904 ; at Covent Garden, July 10th, 1905 ; and in English at the Lyric by the Moody-Manners Company, August, 1907.

feels inclined, Sharpless tries to dissuade him from such a cruel step. Butterfly's voice is heard singing. She appears attended by girl friends. As her relations enter to be present at the forthcoming ceremony, Sharpless, having found out that Butterfly believes in Pinkerton's good faith, again endeavours to dissuade the lieutenant. Refreshments are now handed round, while Butterfly introduces Pinkerton to her relations. Then, while the latter examines the marriage bond, Butterfly tells her lover that she has renounced her old religion for his, throwing away the little images she carried in her loose sleeves. The marriage contract is signed, but before the guests leave, the Bonze, Butterfly's uncle, appears. He has discovered that she has renounced the religion of her own people, and curses her for so doing. He goes off with the relations. The servants bring Butterfly her wedding garment, and the pair are left alone, singing a love-duet as the curtain falls.

The first part of the second Act shows the interior of the house. Three years have elapsed. Butterfly and Suzuki are alone, and while the former is quite confident that Pinkerton has not deserted her, but will return, Suzuki cannot convince herself that this is true. Sharpless now comes in. He has brought with him a letter which is a proof of Pinkerton's desertion; he finds it no easy matter to break the news to Butterfly. At this moment Yamadori enters. He is a wealthy man who wishes to marry Butterfly, for in the Japanese law desertion is equivalent to divorce. Butterfly, in confident belief of Pinkerton's constancy, of course refuses his offer. When he has gone, Sharpless tries again to read the fatal letter. Before he can get to the account of Pinkerton's marriage with an American lady, Butterfly brings out her little son, and the Consul feels how impossible it is to say more. Goro now rouses her to fury by telling her that a boy born under these conditions in America would be treated as an outcast. Soon the two women are left alone, and suddenly the firing of a cannon is heard. It is the signal of an approaching ship. With glasses Butterfly discerns the American flag. It is Pinkerton's ship; he is returning. In great excitement she and Suzuki decorate the room with flowers. Then they and the boy place themselves at the window-screens to watch for Pinkerton's expected arrival. Night falls as the curtain descends.

The second part of the Act shows us at the rise of the curtain Butterfly, Suzuki, and the child still in their position at the screens; only Butterfly is awake and watching. It is morning, Suzuki awakens and persuades Butterfly to go into her room and rest. Pinkerton and Sharpless enter. They explain all to Suzuki, and that the lady waiting outside in the garden is Pinkerton's wife. Suzuki goes out to bring her in. Pinkerton, coward-like, says he cannot bear to see Butterfly, and leaves. Suzuki comes in with Kate, the wife, the latter expressing her wish to take the child and bring him up. Butterfly enters; she guesses who Kate is, says she will give up the boy to Pinkerton, and that he is to come to fetch him in half-an-hour's time. Kate and Sharpless go out. Butterfly in the great agony dismisses Suzuki and prepares to kill herself with a dagger. At this moment Suzuki from without pushes the boy into the room, Butterfly seats him on a stool, placing a flag and a doll in his hands, disappears behind a screen, and presently staggers forward to die as Pinkerton and the others rush in and the curtain falls.

MANON LESCAUT.*

THE libretto of this opera is founded upon the famous work of Abbé Prevost of the same title. The scene of the first Act is laid in Amiens. The exterior of an inn. Edmondo and other students and various citizens are seated at tables, drinking, &c. Des Grieux enters and joins them. Presently the diligence from Arras arrives, from which there descends Lescaut the soldier, Geronte the treasure-general, and Manon, Lescaut's sister. The two men enter the inn to arrange for the night's lodging. Des Grieux is struck by Manon's beauty and speaks to her. She tells him she is on her way to a convent, as her brother calls her; she goes in, saying she will return and speak to him later. Lescaut and Geronte come out from the inn; the former sits down at a card table, while the latter gives orders to the innkeeper, that in an hour's time he requires a carriage and fast horses. Edmondo overhears this conversation, and tells Des Grieux that there is a plot to take Manon off to Paris. When Manon comes out again, Des Grieux resumes his protestations of admiration, tells her that Geronte is planning an abduction, and, when Edmondo comes up to say that the carriage as ordered is now ready, presses her to elope with him. The three go off behind the inn, Des Grieux wearing Edmondo's cloak. Presently Edmondo returns and informs Geronte that the carriage is on its way to Paris. Geronte is in a fury, but Lescaut is indifferent and advises him to have patience, that a student's purse is limited, and that his time will come. They go in to supper as the curtain falls.

The scene of the second Act shows a room in Geronte's house in Paris. Manon is discovered having her hair dressed. Lescaut comes in. In the course of their conversation it is explained that Manon has left Des Grieux to become Geronte's mistress; she is still anxious though to hear of her old lover. She has tired of all the luxury that now surrounds her.

---

* First performed at Turin, Feb. 1st, 1893, and at Covent Garden, May 14th, 1894.

The singers, who now enter and perform a madrigal, please her no more than the performance that follows of a minuet, yet she joins in the latter with Geronte. She is presently left alone, when suddenly Des Grieux appears (Lescaut having previously gone off to bring him). Their scene of reproaches and reconciliation is interrupted by the entrance of Geronte. Geronte controls his anger, and says sarcastically he will leave them, but that he and Manon will meet again. The lovers resume their duet, which is interrupted once again by the entrance of Lescaut, who says that Geronte, in revenge, has denounced Manon and that they must fly. But it is too late. Soldiers enter, and Manon is taken off. There follows an intermezzo, illustrating Manon's imprisonment and journey to Havre.

The scene of the third Act shows a square near the harbour at Havre. Des Grieux and Lescaut are waiting to rescue Manon, who is confined in the adjoining barracks. When the guard is changed, Lescaut taps at the bars of a window. It opens and Manon appears. A duet between the lovers ensues. Meanwhile, Lescaut's plans for the escape have failed, the stage fills with citizens, and presently a picket of soldiers comes out of the barracks escorting a number of women in chains; Manon is among them. The roll call is made, and as women are sent off to the ship in the harbour, Des Grieux passionately implores the captain to let him go too. His request is granted, and the curtain falls as all go off.

The scene of the fourth Act is a vast plain on the borders of the Territory of New Orleans. Manon and Des Grieux are alone. They are worn out with fatigue, and Manon is dying. Des Grieux scans the horizon; there are no signs of water, an arid waste meets his eyes whichever way he turns. Night falls, and presently, overcome by fever and exhaustion, Manon dies, Des Grieux falling in senseless grief upon her body as the curtain falls.

LA TOSCA.*

THE libretto of this opera is founded on Sardou's play by Signori Illica and Giacosa. The scene of the first Act is the interior of the church of Sant' Andrea alla Valle, Rome. Angelotti, a consul of the discredited Roman Republic, has escaped from Fort San Angelo. He enters the building, and, finding the key of a side-chapel, previously hidden for his use by his sister, disappears through the chapel gate. The sacristan enters, and after him Mario Cavaradossi, a painter, who is working at a picture representing Mary Magdalen—it is a portrait of the

---

* First performed at Rome, Jan. 14th, 1900; in London, at Covent Garden, July 12th, the same year.

Marchesa Attavanti, Angelotti's sister. As he paints he compares the blue eyes and light colouring with the dark beauty of Tosca, the celebrated singer, of whom he is enamoured. Presently, Angelotti reappears from the chapel. Tosca's voice, calling " Mario," is heard from without. Hurriedly the painter gives Angelotti a basket containing food, and urges him back into his hiding-place. Tosca enters; she is agitated and jealous, thinking that her lover has been talking to some woman. The painter calms her, but on her seeing the portrait she is again suspicious, but Cavaradossi succeeds in mollifying her and she goes out. Once more Angelotti appears, and taking some clothes for a disguise which his sister had left concealed for him, makes his exit with instructions from Cavaradossi how to find his way to the latter's villa, where he can be concealed. The chorus now enter acclaiming the defeat of Buonaparte and announcing the gala performance to be held that evening. Tosca is to sing in a new cantata. Scarpia, chief of the police, Spoletta, and other police agents enter. They are searching for Angelotti. In the chapel, suspiciously unlocked, Scarpia finds a fan with the Attavanti arms upon it. The picture upon the easel convinces him that Angelotti's escape has been achieved with the aid of his sister and Cavaradossi. Tosca comes in again. By means of the fan her jealous feelings are once more roused by Scarpia, who is greatly attracted by her beauty, and as she goes off to Cavaradossi's villa, thinking to find the Attavanti there, she is followed by Spoletta acting upon Scarpia's orders. As the cardinal and worshippers enter the church, Scarpia declares his double intention of recapturing Angelotti and possessing himself of Tosca.

The second Act shows us Scarpia's apartments on an upper floor of the Farnese Palace. Night; the table laid for supper. Scarpia orders Sciarrone, a gendarme, to take a note to Tosca, saying he wishes to see her after the cantata has been sung. Spoletta enters, and says he followed Tosca to Cavaradossi's villa, failed to find Angelotti, but has brought back the painter under arrest. The painter denies having helped Angelotti to escape. Tosca's voice is heard in the distance singing her part in the cantata. She presently enters, and on Cavaradossi being taken into an inner room—the torture-chamber— there ensues a scene between her and Scarpia, in which the latter finally forces her to say where Angelotti is concealed, the only terms on which he will consent to release the painter from the torture. When she says, " The well in the garden," Cavaradossi is brought in bleeding in a swoon. He revives, to hear with horror that Tosca has been forced to betray him. At this moment Sciarrone enters to say that Buonaparte has fought a successful battle. A cry of enthusiasm from Cavaradossi is followed by his being taken off for execution. Tosca is held back by Scarpia, and in the following scene, if she will give herself to him, he promises that her lover shall be saved. This is to be done by carrying out the execution formally, but with blank cartridge, that Cavaradossi is to feign death, and to be subsequently allowed to escape. When Tosca agrees, these orders are given to Spoletta, but as Scarpia goes to the writing-table to make out a safe-conduct for her, she carefully conceals a knife lying on the supper-table, and when he approaches her, she suddenly stabs him through the heart.

The scene of the last Act is a platform of the Castle San Angelo; the Tiber flows below the battlements at the back, and in the distance can be seen St. Peter's and the Vatican. Night; a shepherd's voice is heard singing afar; and as the dawn comes there is a great clanging of the church bells of the city. Cavaradossi is brought in. He is allowed to write a letter of farewell to Tosca; while doing so, she herself comes in and explains the plan for his escape. As the clock strikes four, the firing-party enter. Cavaradossi is placed in position, the soldiers fire, and he falls. Tosca finds to her horror that Scarpia had deceived her—the execution was a real one after all. As Spoletta and others enter to arrest her for the murder of Scarpia she throws herself over the parapet into the Tiber.

ROSSINI.

GIOACCHINO ANTONIO ROSSINI was born on Feb. 29th, 1792, at Pesara, in Italy. His father, Giuseppe Rossini, was a player upon the horn, and his mother, Anna Giudarini, a chorus singer in the opera. The Rossinis, father and mother, were accustomed during the opera season to go wherever they could get work, and when that was over would return to Pesara, living on the money they had made until the following season. By this means their boy Gioacchino, who at an early age showed great talent for music, had a continuous change and variety of masters.

Musicians, like doctors, and other members of scientific professions, almost invariably disagree, or, shall I say, hold different opinions, and so young Rossini made but small progress in the science of music during his early childhood. In the year 1804 his parents placed him definitely under the tuition of Angelo Tesei, at Bologna, who taught him the piano and singing, he having a very fine voice as a boy. On March 20th, 1807, Rossini was admitted as student to the Lyceum of the same town, where he received lessons in composition, &c., from Mattei.

His first operatic production was entitled "La Cambiale di matrimonio," which was played at the Theatre San Mosè, at Venice, in the autumn of the year 1810. He married, March 15th, 1822, at Castenaso, near Bologna, Isabella Angela Colbran, prima donna of the Theatre Royal, Naples, and daughter of Gianni Colbran, musician of the chapel to the King of Spain. She died at Bologna, Oct. 7th, 1845.

Rossini was Associate of the Académie des Beaux-Arts of Paris, and honorary member of a great number of academies and musical societies. He was also one of the thirty foreign members of the Order of Merit of Prussia, and Commander and Knight of many other Orders. He died Nov. 13th, 1868, having attained to the ripe age of seventy-six years, and was buried Nov. 21st, at Paris.

IL BARBIERE DI SIVIGLIA.*

THE scene opens in a street in Seville. It is dawn, and the Count Almaviva, with musicians, serenades his mistress, Rosina, the ward of

---

* Was written for the Theatre Argentina, Rome, where it was produced in the year 1816. First performed in London at the King's Theatre, Jan. 27th, 1818.
Maria Felicita Malibran made her first appearance in London on June 17th, 1825, in the *rôle* of Rosina.

Doctor Bartolo. Figaro appears upon the scene. He is the barber and factotum of the town, who busies himself in everybody's affairs. The Count has just divulged to him his passion for Rosina, when she appears upon the balcony. Bartolo, her guardian, also steps out, but by a ruse Rosina gets rid of him, and succeeds in dropping a note to the Count in the street. The Count then endeavours to obtain an interview with Rosina in the disguise of a drunken soldier. He forces himself into Bartolo's home, claiming lodging under an order for billet, but Bartolo sends for the police and gives him into custody.

In the second Act the Count enters Bartolo's home as a music-master, affirming that Doctor Basilio, Rosina's music-master, is ill, and has sent him, his pupil, in his place. Bartolo is suspicious of him, but the Count gives him Rosina's letter to himself, suggesting that Rosina should be made to believe it was written by another lady to the Count, and so be induced to give him up. The barber also comes in to shave the Doctor, and succeeds in getting from him the key of the balcony, with a view to the elopement of Rosina with the Count. Basilio, however, arrives, and is with some difficulty got rid of, since he scarcely believes the assurances of the Count, Figaro, and Rosina that he is looking very ill. The barber then shaves Bartolo, the Count and Rosina meanwhile laying their plans under cover of the music lesson. But the Doctor finds them out, and Basilio again appears, and assures the Doctor he knows nothing of any pupil, and that he never sent the Count to take his place. Bartolo is very angry, for he himself means to marry his ward, Rosina, and has taken Basilio into his confidence on the subject. He craftily uses the letter the Count gave him to create suspicion in her mind, assures her she is deceived, and induces her to consent to marry her guardian himself.

Figaro and the Count come, as arranged, to the verandah by night to take Rosina with them, but she repulses the Count. The mistake, however, is explained, and they prepare to descend by the ladder, to the air " Zitti Zitti," when it is discovered that some one has removed the ladder. Basilio comes in with a notary and marriage contract, and under the joint persuasion of a ring given to him by the Count, and a threat of a bullet if he refuses, he stands by while the Count and Rosina sign the contract. Doctor Bartolo arrives with the police just too late to prevent the Count's success, but becomes rapidly reconciled to the inevitable, and gives them his blessing.

GUILLAUME TELL.*

WILLIAM TELL is discovered leaning on his bow. The Swiss peasants are rejoicing at a marriage festival, but Tell laments the condition of his country. Arnold, a young Swiss, the son of the patriarch Melcthal, is in love with Matilda, the daughter of Rudolpho, Captain of the Guard of the tyrant Gessler, the German Governor, and he discloses to Tell his fatal affection for the daughter of one of their country's enemies. In the midst of the nuptial rejoicings Leuthold appears—a peasant who has killed an agent of Gessler, who was insulting his daughter. There is no escape for him but by crossing the lake in a storm. None of the fishermen dare take him across, but Tell does so. The first Act closes with Gessler's soldiers trying to discover who has assisted Leuthold to escape. They take Melcthal prisoner.

In the next Act Arnold meets Matilda, and their love-scene is interrupted by Tell, who accuses him of being false to his country, and tells him that Gessler has put his father, Melcthal, to death. Arnold is inspired with hate of Gessler for the deed, and vows to avenge his father's death. This Act closes with the gathering of the inhabitants of the various cantons to rescue their country from the Germans by arms. Matilda and Arnold meet again, when Arnold tells her that he must forsake her until his father's death is avenged.

The scene changes to the square of Altorf. Gessler has erected a pole, on which is his cap. The populace are required to salute it. Tell approaches, and refuses to do so. His son Jemmy is with him. Gessler notices the son, and orders Tell to shoot the apple from his son's head, otherwise his son will be killed. Then follows the scene of the shooting, in which Tell is successful; but Gessler is only the more infuriated, and has him made prisoner. With difficulty Matilda succeeds in interposing for the safety of Jemmy.

In the last Act Arnold is roused by the peasants to lead them to the rescue of Tell, and to vengeance on Gessler. He obeys the summons, and the scene changes to the lake of the four cantons. Here is Tell's wife. Matilda enters with Jemmy, and while the three are talking, Tell arrives with Arnold, amid the shouts of victory. Gessler has fallen by Tell's arrow, which he produces, and liberty is insured to Switzerland.

---

* Was first produced at the Opera House, Paris, August 3rd, 1829 ; in London, in an English version, "arranged" by Bishop, May 1st, 1830, and in French, Dec. 3rd, 1838.

SMETANA.

FRIEDERICH SMETANA, the distinguished Bohemian composer, and, it is interesting to note, the teacher of Antonin Dvorák, was born in Bohemia, March 2nd, 1824. For a short time he studied under Liszt, becoming a pianist of no small repute. In 1866 he was appointed conductor of the National Theatre at Prague, holding this post until 1874, when increasing deafness compelled his resignation. He died May 12th, 1884. As a composer he is known in England by some of his symphonic poems, and one of his many operas, "Die Verkaufte Braut." This work was composed in 1866, but was not given outside his native country till its production at Vienna in 1890. It was first heard in London in 1895. Its overture is a familiar and charming work, often to be heard at orchestral concerts.

DIE VERKAUFTE BRAUT.

THE scene of this comic opera, "The Bartered Bride," is laid in Bohemia. The action of the first Act takes place in a village square at the time of the Church Consecration Festival in the spring. Marie, the daughter of a peasant and his wife, Kruschina and Katrinka, is in love with Hans, a young man, who is really the eldest son of Micha, a wealthy farmer, though in the opening scene with her he only tells her that his father had married twice, and that he had been driven from home by his mother-in-law. Kezal, a marriage broker, induces the parents to betroth Marie, against her will, to the rich younger son of Micha, Wenzel by name, saying that he believes the elder to be dead.

In the second Act, the scene of which is the village inn, Wenzel and Marie have an interview, in which, disguising her identity, she says that the girl Marie he is betrothed to loves another, and is, in fact, a coquette, but that she knows of another girl just as pretty, who is in love with him, indicating that it is no other than herself. Wenzel says he will have nothing to do with the bride proposed for him. Kezal enters with Hans, and persuades him by a bribe of 300 crowns to give up Marie. Hans agrees, on condition that Marie marries no other than Micha's son. Kezal presently returns with the agreement drawn up, and the villagers are indignant at Hans' supposed perfidy.

The third Act begins with the arrival of a group of strolling players, amongst whom is Esmeralda, a beautiful dancer. She induces Wenzel, who is attracted by her charms, to take the part of the performing bear, as the man who does so is drunk, and the fame of the show is at stake. Wenzel then tells his parents, Micha and Agnes, that he has heard that Marie is a coquette, and that in consequence he will not marry her. Marie is now told by her father and mother that Hans has been faithless. Wenzel recognizes her as the girl whom he had met in the morning, and agrees to marry her. Marie, on being left alone to make up her mind, has an angry scene with Hans. Hans does not explain what he has done, but all is made clear when he is recognized as being Micha's long-lost eldest son. Kezal is laughed at, and the opera ends with Wenzel, dressed up as a bear, being taken off by his mother, and Micha's blessing on "the bartered bride."

TCHAIKOVSKY.

PETER ILICH TCHAIKOVSKY, in some ways the greatest of the modern school of Russian composers, was born in 1840, at Wotkinsk, in the Ural district, his father being an engineer in the Imperial mines. He studied jurisprudence, and was appointed to a post in the Ministry of Justice, until in 1862, when the Conservatoire of Music was opened in Petersburg, he entered himself there as a student of music. In 1866 he was appointed professor of harmony and counterpoint at the Moscow Conservatoire, holding that post for twelve years. From 1878 he devoted himself entirely to composition. In 1892 the University of Cambridge conferred on him the degree of Doctor of Music, although he had previously visited England, and conducted works at the Philharmonic Concerts. He died October, 1893. Best known in England by his orchestral music, he wrote several operas, the only one of which to reach this country being—

EUGENE ONIEGIN.*

THE libretto of this opera is founded upon the poem of the Russian poet, Pushkin. Act I. opens with a scene representing a garden in front of Mme. Larina's house. She is the widow of a landed proprietor, and has two daughters, Tatiana and Olga. As the curtain rises the voices of the two girls are heard singing through the open door of the house. The mother and nurse are in conversation when there enter peasants bearing harvest offerings. There ensues a dance, and presently Tatiana and Olga appear. In the conversation that follows, it is shown that the characters of the two girls differ widely, Tatiana being romantic and emotional, while her sister is of a more lively and careless disposition. Soon Lenski, a young poet, betrothed to Olga, comes in with his friend, Eugene Oniegin, whom he introduces. The party breaks up into pairs, and it is shown that Oniegin and Tatiana are attracted by each other. Evening comes on, and as all go into the house the curtain falls. In the second scene Tatiana is in her own room preparing for bed. She has fallen violently in love with Oniegin, and is compelled to write a letter to him, in which she confesses it. With daybreak the nurse enters, surprised to find Tatiana still undressed ; Tatiana gives

---

* First performed at Moscow, March, 1879 ; in England, at the New Olympic Theatre, Oct. 17th, 1892.

her the letter to deliver to Oniegin. The third scene is part of the garden. Oniegin and Tatiana have a duet, in which the former says he has received Tatiana's letter, but that he does not care for her enough to marry her. The first scene of the second Act is the ball-room in the house of the Larinas. Oniegin finds the entertainment wearisome, and to pay out Lenski for having brought him to it, he dances and flirts with Olga. When Lenski expostulates with Olga, she is angry with him for his jealousy, and engages herself to Oniegin for the cotillon. Here M. Triquet, a French tutor, sings a song in honour of Tatiana's birthday. A mazurka is now played for the cotillon. Meanwhile Oniegin and Lenski quarrel ; there is nothing for it but a duel. This takes place in the next scene on the banks of a river. After an aria for Lenski, Oniegin enters, the duel takes place, and Lenski is killed. The third and last Act begins with another ball-room scene, in the house of a rich nobleman in Petersburg. Oniegin has an aria expressing the general aimlessness of his life. Princess Gremin enters, she is Tatiana now married. Oniegin discovers that he loves her now that it is too late. In the final scene, a drawing-room in Prince Gremin's house, Oniegin enters to Tatiana, and implores her to accept his love, but it is in vain. Tatiana remains true to her husband, although she has never ceased to care for Oniegin, and as the curtain falls she goes out, leaving him overcome with despair.

THOMAS.

CHARLES LOUIS AMBROISE THOMAS, son of a well-known professor of music at Metz, was born in that town on Aug. 5th, 1811. He entered the Conservatoire, Paris, in 1828, being then somewhat advanced in his musical education, owing to his father's care. He studied the pianoforte under Zimmerman, harmony and accompaniment under Dourlen, and composition under Lesueur. He gained the following prizes at the Conservatoire:—1829, First Prize as a Pianist; 1830, First Prize for Harmony; and in 1832, the Grand Prize of Rome. In 1851 Thomas was made a Member of the Académie des Beaux-Arts; December, 1869, Officer d'Instruction Publique; 1871, he succeeded Auber as director of the Conservatoire de Musique; and in 1868 he was made Commander of the Legion of Honour. He died at Paris, Feb. 12th, 1896.

MIGNON.*

THE curtain rises upon the courtyard of a German inn. Country folk are drinking, when Lothario, an old man upon his travels, enters, and sings a mournful air. He is in search of his daughter Mignon, who in her childhood was stolen from her home by the gipsies. At the same inn is a company of gipsies, with whom is Mignon, who offers to amuse the guests staying at the inn. Mignon is told to dance, and when she refuses, is rescued from the brutality of the chief of the gipsies by Lothario, who, however, does not recognize in her his own lost daughter, and by Guglielmo, a young fresh man from the university, who is travelling for pleasure, and arrives opportunely on the scene. Mignon falls in love with Guglielmo, and persuades him to let her accompany him, he having first purchased her liberty from the gipsies. But there is also staying at the inn a company of strolling actors. Filina, their prima donna, seeing Guglielmo, determines to fascinate him, and succeeds in doing so, persuading him, moreover, to accompany the troupe to the castle of a Baron in the neighbourhood, where the actors

---

* Founded, of course, upon Goethe's famous "Wilhelm Meister." It was produced in Paris, in 1866, and in London, at Drury Lane, July 5th, 1870.

are about to perform. Thither Mignon follows him, and, deeply hurt by Guglielmo's apparent affection for Filina, is on the point of throwing herself into the lake, when Lothario, who has also wandered to the castle, rushes from the trees on the bank just in time to save her from drowning herself. In her despair Mignon imprecates the vengeance of heaven on the occupiers of the castle, and unguardedly expresses a wish that it may be burnt to the ground. Lothario takes the hint in earnest, and sets fire to the building. Mignon is with difficulty rescued from the flames by Guglielmo, Filina having purposely sent Mignon back into the castle to fetch her bouquet. The second Act ends with a tableau of this crisis in the play, the curtain falling upon Guglielmo holding the fainting Mignon in his arms, after her second escape from peril.

VERDI.

GIUSEPPE VERDI was born at Roncole, in the Duchy of Parma, on Oct. 10th, 1813. His father was an innkeeper of that town. He received his first lessons in music from an organist at Milan (where he was living), 1833 to 1836. Afterwards he studied under Lavinga, and on Nov. 17th, 1839, produced his first musical drama, entitled "Oberto di San Bonifazio," at La Scala, Milan. In the year 1867 his opera "Don Carlos" was produced at the Royal Italian Opera House, Covent Garden; 1847, "I Masnadieri," which he had written for Her Majesty's Theatre, London, was there performed, Jenny Lind taking the part of heroine. The following is a list of honours conferred upon this remarkably popular composer:—Member of the Legion of Honour and Corresponding Member of the Académie des Beaux-Arts, Dec. 10th, 1859. In 1861 he was elected a Member of the Italian Parliament; 1862, Grand Cross of the Russian Order of St. Stanislaus; 1864, June 15th, Foreign Associate of the Académie des Beaux-Arts; 1872, Grand Officer of the Order of the Crown of Italy; and in the same year the Viceroy of Egypt conferred on him the Order of Osmain; Nov. 22nd, 1874, Italian Senator, by decree; May, 1875, Commander of the Legion of Honour; and the same year he was given the Cross of Commander and Star of the Austrian Order of Franz Joseph. The change in style in his last dramatic works, "Otello" and "Falstaff," from the earlier ones was a fine example of an impressionability to change and progress in the art that is only too rarely shown. It must be remember, too, that Verdi was eighty years of age when "Falstaff" was produced. He died Jan. 27th, 1901.

AÏDA.*

THE era of this opera is somewhat early, being during one of the reigns of the innumerable Pharaohs, kings of Egypt. Prior to the commencement of the opera, Aïda, daughter of Amonasro, King of Ethiopia, has been taken prisoner by the Egyptians, and given to Amneris, daughter of Pharaoh, King of Egypt. She takes a great fancy to her, but, unfortun-

---

* Was first performed at Cairo, December, 1871, and in Italy, at Milan, February, 1872, and was heard in London, at Covent Garden, on June 22nd, 1876. Edouard de Reszke made his *début* in this opera in Paris, April 22nd, 1876.

ately, Radames, Captain of the King's Guard—whom Amneris secretly loves—does the same thing, and falls desperately in love with Aïda.

The first scene is a hall in the palace of the King of Egypt at Memphis. Radames and Ramphis, high priest of Isis, are talking over the fact that the Ethiopians, led by their king, are about to invade Egypt, and the priest hints that Radames has been selected as general of the forces of Isis. An interview then follows between Radames, Amneris, and Aïda, in which it is evident to the jealous daughter of the King that her slave and Radames love one another, and she secretly vows to be revenged. The King then declares that Isis has selected his former Captain of Guards as general of the forces, and he is given the standard by Amneris. The Act ends with Radames undergoing a mysterious ceremony in the Temple of Isis before leaving for the seat of war.

The first scene of the next Act is a hall in the apartments of Amneris. The Egyptians are returning victorious, and her slaves are bedecking their mistress for the grand festival which is to take place. On the slaves retiring, Aïda enters, and Amneris, by telling her that Radames has been slain, wrings from her the fact that she loves him; then, declaring her statement to be false, and that Radames really lives, and is returning to be crowned by her, she vows to have revenge on Aïda for daring to look upon her lover.

The next scene is the entrance-gate of Thebes. The King is on a temporary throne, with his daughter by his side, and a large multitude of people are assembled to welcome back their victorious countrymen. The army then marches in, led by Radames, who, after being crowned with laurels by Amneris, is told to ask a boon by the King. He begs that the Ethiopian prisoners be set at liberty, and among them Amonasro, Aïda's father. His request is granted, excepting Amonasro, who is detained as security for the good behaviour of his subjects. The King then presents Radames with the hand of his daughter Amneris, and with this ends the second Act.

The third Act opens with a scene on the banks of the Nile. On the summit of a rock is the temple of Isis, from which proceeds the sounds of a chorus of priests and priestesses singing to the honour of the goddess. Ramphis and Amneris, accompanied by her women, enter the temple. Aïda then appears thickly veiled, having an appointment with Radames. Suddenly her father, Amonasro, enters, and begs her to get her lover to say which road the Egyptian troops have guarded, as the Ethiopians are about to make another attack on Thebes. She at first treats his proposal with scorn, but at length gives way; and on Radames entering, Amonasro hides. Aïda prays her lover to fly with her to her native land, pointing out to him that if he remains in Thebes he must marry Amneris, and lose her for ever. On his consenting to do so, she asks him which road they can escape by without meeting the Egyptian forces. He tells her the gorges of Napata, and so lets out the secret to Amonasro, who, rushing from his hiding-place, declares that there he will plant his forces. They are all three about to leave, when Amneris and Ramphis, with priests and guards, coming out of the temple, accuse them of treachery. Amonasro attempts to stab Amneris, but is prevented by Radames, who, giving himself up as prisoner, tells Aïda and her father to escape.

The opening scene of the last Act is a hall lying between the Hall of Justice and the prison in which Radames is confined. Amneris is discovered in despair at the fate of her lover. She calls on the guard to bring him before her, and on his entrance she prays him to clear himself before his judges, and so live to share her love. He refuses, declaring that now Aïda is dead he has nothing to live for. Amneris tells him that Aïda is not dead, for although the Ethiopians were again overcome, and the King Amonasro slain, yet Aïda escaped no one knows whither; but he still declares he will not live to marry her, and so is led back to prison. Amneris falls back in her chair overcome with grief. The priests are then seen to cross over to the Hall of Justice, and Radames follows, surrounded by a guard. Ramphis, the high priest, accuses him of being a traitor to his country, and on his answering nothing, he passes sentence upon him, to be buried alive in a vault in the temple of Vulcan. On this, Amneris rushes wildly in, calling down the vengeance of Heaven on them if they do not alter the sentence, but the priests are obdurate.

The last scene is the temple of Vulcan, so constructed that both the temple and the vault are shown. Radames is discovered in the latter, and a crowd of priests, &c., in the temple. Suddenly Aïda appears in the vault. She tells her lover that, guessing what his fate would be, she has, unseen, come to share his fate. Amneris is seen to enter the temple, and, throwing herself on the stone over the vault, prays the gods to receive the soul of her lover.

UN BALLO IN MASCHERA.*

THE scene of this opera is laid in Boston in America. Richard, Earl of Warwick, Governor of Boston, becomes enamoured of Amelia, wife of his secretary, Renato, a creole, and she, though deploring it, has more than a tender feeling for him.

---

* Was written for Naples in the year 1858, but, for political reasons, was not allowed to be performed. It was produced the following year with an altered text that did not offend the authorities, at the Theatre Apollo, Rome, and in London, at the Lyceum, June 15th. 1861.

In the first Act, Thomas and Samuel, two conspirators, are discovered plotting to take the life of the Governor, of which he is warned by his faithful secretary, Renato. An application is made to Richard to banish one Ulrica, a fortune-teller, but he determines first to pay her a visit incognito with his attendants ; for this purpose he disguises himself as a fisherman. While there, Amelia comes seeking an interview with the sybil. The hut is cleared, but Richard hides himself, and overhears his ladylove ask Ulrica for a charm against her unlawful passion for himself. She is told to pluck, at the hour of midnight, a certain herb that grows at the place of execution. On her leaving, the attendants of the Earl are admitted, and he, stealing from his hiding place, joins them unnoticed. Demanding of Ulrica his fortune, she tells him his best friend will shortly take his life ; and further states that he who first shakes him by the hand will be the man. Richard offers his hand to all in the hut ; none will take it. At this moment Renato enters, who at once grasps it, and in doing in so, recognizes his master, much to Ulrica's astonishment.

The next scene is the place of execution, outside the walls of Boston, at midnight. Amelia, heavily veiled, has come to pluck the herb, when Richard suddenly appears, and presses his suit. Hearing footsteps approaching she again drops her veil. It is Renato, her husband, who begs the Governor to fly, as the conspirators are on his track. He only consents to do so on Renato promising to lead the veiled lady to the city without asking who she is. Hardly has Richard left before the conspirators enter, headed by Thomas and Samuel, and demand Amelia to unveil. Renato is about to protect her at the point of his sword, when she rushes in between the combatants, and in doing so her veil falls off, disclosing to the secretary his wife. Renato, justly incensed, joins the plot against the Governor's life, and the lot falls upon him to do the deed. Meanwhile, Richard, repenting of his underhand attempts against the honour of his faithful servant's wife, determines to get rid of the temptation by giving Renato a good appointment in Arragon, and sending him there with his wife.

The last scene is the masked ball. Amelia is warning Richard of the attempt that will be made upon his life, when Renato steps between them and stabs him to the heart. The Earl then declares Amelia to be innocent, hands Renato the order for his departure with his wife, and, forgiving all, dies.

ERNANI.*

ERNANI is in reality son and heir of the Duke of Legorbia and Cardona, proscribed and pursued by Don Carlos Quinto, King of Castile, but has assumed the name of Ernani and the leadership of a body of brigands in the Sierras.

The scene opens in the mountains of Arragon, where his followers are drinking and enjoying themselves. In the distance is the Castle of Don Ruy Gomez de Silva, with whose niece, Elvira, Ernani is in love. Ernani and his companions vow to rescue Elvira from her uncle, who is an old man, and is on the point of insisting upon marrying his niece.

The scene changes to Elvira's room in the Castle. It is the night before her wedding. But the King, Don Carlos, is also enamoured of Elvira. This very night he seeks an interview with her, and is about to take her away, when Ernani appears on the scene. They quarrel, but are interrupted by Don Silva and his servants. The King is recognized, and has then to appease Don Silva by pretending he had come in disguise to his castle to confer with him respecting his approaching election to the Empire. Ernani is permitted to go. Silva is within an hour of being married to Elvira, when Ernani gains admission to his castle as a pilgrim, and is promised hospitality. He is flying from the King's soldiers, and Silva offers to preserve him. Ernani tells him who he is. Silva goes to fortify the ramparts, and returns to the room just in time to witness an affectionate scene between Elvira and Ernani. The King is at the gate, and to keep Ernani for his own revenge, Silva conceals him in a secret passage. The King enters, and demands Ernani. Silva refuses to give him up. The King threatens his life, but Elvira entering, he offers to take her instead of her uncle, and does so. Silva then takes two swords and would fight with Ernani, who, however, shows him that the King is his rival for Elvira, and they both vow vengeance first on the King, after that Ernani swears most solemnly to give up his life to Silva when he demands it.

The third Act takes place in the vaults of Aix-la-Chapelle, near Charlemagne's tomb. Here the conspirators against the election of Don Carlos to the Empire are assembled. The lot falls to assassinate the King; but the King has heard of the place of meeting, and discloses himself just as he is elected Emperor Charles V. A procession of electors and courtiers comes to the vault to congratulate him. The conspirators are

---

* Was produced at Venice in the month of March, 1844 ; in England, at Her Majesty's Theatre, March 8th, 1845. Pauline Lucca made her *début* in the opera at Olmëtz, in September, 1859. On July 18th, 1863, she first appeared at Covent Garden Theatre, in the opera " Vasco di Gama."

doomed, and Ernani having disclosed the fact that he is in reality John of Arragon, Elvira intercedes with the Emperor, who pardons them, and gives Elvira to Ernani. They are married, but on the very evening of the wedding Silva appears, blows the horn which Ernani had given him as a pledge of his oath, and demands Ernani's life. In this awful crisis Ernani remains true to his word, and stabs himself. Elvira falls fainting on his body, while Silva exults in his revenge.

FALSTAFF.*

"FALSTAFF," the last of Verdi's operas, has for hero the familiar Sir John of the "Merry Wives" and "Henry IV." Boïto, the librettist, has made a very clever operatic version. The first scene of Act I. is a room in the Garter Inn.

Falstaff has just sealed two letters, when Dr. Caius enters complaining that while drinking with Bardolph and Pistol they robbed him. He gets no sympathy from the knight, and is escorted out by his late companions. Falstaff now learns that he has no money to pay the bill of the host of the Garter Inn, and tells Bardolph and Pistol how he intends to make love to Mrs. Ford and Mrs. Page, handing them the letters to deliver. They both refuse to do this, saying their honour forbids it. Falstaff calls in a page to take them, and then delivers his famous discourse upon Honour.

The second scene is laid in a garden in front of Ford's house. Mrs. Ford and Mrs. Page compare the letters which have arrived, and they plot with Nannette (Ann Page, but in this version made the daughter of Mrs. Ford) and Dame Quickly how to punish their sender. They go off behind the trees while Ford, Caius, Bardolph, and Pistol come in. Falstaff's servants betray to Ford the fact that he has sent a letter to his wife. The four women reappear, and the men, except Fenton, go out. Nannette is then left for a moment with Fenton. They exchange kisses and quickly separate as the three others enter, and decide to send a message to Sir John. Again the young lovers are left alone, and then the four men come in once more. Ford decides to have an interview with Falstaff, and Bardolph is to arrange it, Ford to be announced under an assumed name.

In the first scene of the second Act (the Garter Inn once more), Dame Quickly arrives, and says that Mrs. Ford sends word that her husband is away from home daily from two until three. Falstaff say he will

---

* First produced at Milan, Feb. 9th, 1893 ; at Covent Garden, May 19th, 1894.

come. Ford enters, now calling himself Mr. Brook, asks for the knight's assistance in an affair of love ; he cannot succeed in winning the affections of a certain Mistress Ford. He is then amazed to learn that Falstaff is to see her that very day. Falstaff pockets Ford's bag of money and promises to prepare the way with the lady, and goes off. Ford is left in a state of bewilderment and jealous alarm. Falstaff reappears in smart clothing, ready for the appointment, and the curtain falls on the amusing situation of the pair ceremoniously yielding precedence to one another at the door, finally making their exit arm-in-arm The second scene is a room in Ford's house. Dame Quickly explains the result of her interview with Falstaff. A dialogue ensues between Mrs. Ford and Nannette, the latter saying that Mr. Ford insists on her marrying Dr. Caius. The mother promises to prevent it. Servants bring in the basket of dirty linen. It is placed behind a screen. Mrs. Ford is left alone, and Falstaff enters. The duet is interrupted by Dame Quickly announcing the arrival of Mrs. Page. Falstaff hurriedly steps behind the screen. Mrs. Page enters with the news that Ford is coming —a surprise to all. Falstaff is thereupon completely hidden by the screen being folded round him. Ford, Fenton, and Caius enter. The house is to be searched from top to bottom. When the women are left, Falstaff is placed in the basket. The men enter again, searching wildly everywhere only to find Nannette and Fenton, who had taken advantage of the screen to exchange a kiss. The curtain falls on the throwing of the basket with Falstaff inside out of the window.

The third Act is also divided into two scenes, the first of which is the exterior of the Garter Inn. Falstaff is brooding over his injuries. Dame Quickly enters and eventually is able to pacify him, bringing him a letter which says that Mrs. Ford will await him in the forest; that he is to come at midnight disguised as Herne the Hunter. Mrs. Ford, Mrs. Page, Nannette, Ford, Caius, and Fenton are watching the interview unobserved. Falstaff and Dame Quickly enter the inn. The others plan how Falstaff is to tricked. Nannette to be disguised as the Queen of the Fairies, in white ; Mrs. Page, in green, as a woodland nymph ; Dame Quickly as an enchantress. Ford arranges with Caius how he and Nannette shall be brought together and betrothed, telling Caius to wear a cowl. This Dame Quickly, having come out of the inn, overhears. The second scene is the forest, Herne's Oak in full view. Fenton sings a love-strain, but just as Nannette enters in her fairy dress, Mrs. Ford appears and makes him put on a monk's dress. This is to outwit Ford and Caius. They all go off, and Falstaff appears wearing the antlers. To him enters Mrs. Ford. The voice of Mrs. Page is heard crying out, " Here come the witches." Nannette's fairy invocation is heard, and all the characters in disguise and a troop of fairies come in. There is a dance ; goblins and demons,

appear dancing round Falstaff, pinching him and flogging him with
nettles. The end soon comes. Fenton and Nannette escape together.
Caius is led to think that Bardolph, whom Dame Quickly disguises in
white, is Nannette, but out of the confusion peace is at length made with
Ford forgiving Nannette and consenting to her marriage with Fenton,
all joining in a joyful fugue as finale.

OTELLO.*

THE libretto is founded by Boïto on Shakespeare's tragedy. The scene
of the first Act shows a tavern on a quay-side. Evening; a storm is
raging. Othello's ship is descried, and presently the Moor arrives safely.
He has returned victorious from the battle with the Turks, and enters
the adjoining castle in triumph. Iago tells Roderigo that he will help
him to secure the affections of Desdemona, and that he hates Othello,
who has favoured Cassio rather than himself in the matter of military
promotion. There follows the drinking scene in which Cassio is made
intoxicated and fights with Montano. Confusion ensues, quelled by the
entry of Othello. The latter deprives Cassio of his lieutenancy, to Iago's
great satisfaction. The stage is emptied except for Othello and
Desdemona, and the curtain falls on a love duet.

The scene of the second Act is a hall in the castle. Through a glass
partition at the back is seen a large garden. Iago counsels Cassio to
obtain Desdemona's help in re-instating himself in Othello's favour, and
then delivers the famous "Credo," an expression of his belief in fate driving him to whatever evil may come his way; that faith and heaven are
but inventions. Through the glass at the back Cassio is seen talking to
Desdemona. Othello enters, and Iago makes him begin to have suspicions
of Cassio and his wife. An episode follows, when Cypriotes are seen
bringing Desdemona flowers in the garden. Desdemona then comes into
the hall followed by Emilia. Othello's feelings of jealousy are again
aroused when Desdemona begins to plead on Cassio's behalf. She drops
her handkerchief; Emilia picks it up, and Iago seizes it from her. The
women go out, and Iago suggests further reasons for Othello's growing
belief in Desdemona's unfaithfulness, and the curtain falls on the Moor
vowing vengeance, in which vow Iago joins.

The great hall of the castle is the scene of the third Act, which begins
with Iago pointing out how Othello by hiding behind the pillars will be
able to observe proofs of Cassio's guilt. Othello is left alone, to him

---

* Produced at La Scala, Milan, Feb. 5th, 1887 ; in London, at the Lyceum, July 5th,
1889.

enters Desdemona, and he denounces her for her supposed unfaithfulness. When she has gone Iago enters, and presently Cassio, upon which Othello takes his place behind the pillars. Iago so manages the conversation between him and Cassio that all that Othello hears only adds to his belief. Desdemona's stolen handkerchief is produced, found by Cassio in his room, and Othello recognizes it as the one he gave his wife. Cassio goes out. Iago says to Othello it were best to strangle Desdemona rather than poison her, as the latter suggests, and that he himself will account for Cassio. Othello makes him his lieutenant, as ambassadors enter bringing an order for Othello's recall, and the appointment of Cassio in his place. In the ensuing ensemble Iago advises Othello to take his vengeance quickly, and tells Roderigo his chances are not over if he can secure the death of Cassio. Othello, mad with rage and jealousy, orders everyone out, and falls in a swoon upon the stage. The chorus without are heard singing "Long live Othello! Hail to the Lion of Venice!" as Iago stands pointing with horrible triumph to the prostate body and saying, " See here the Lion! " and the curtain falls.

The scene of the fourth and last Act is Desdemona's bedroom. Desdemona and Emilia are alone. As the former is preparing for bed she sings the "Willow Song," and, as though influenced by a foreboding of disaster, bids Emilia farewell, giving her a ring. After a prayer to the Virgin, Desdemona lays herself down on the bed. Othello enters, finds her asleep; his passions are arrested for the moment; he kisses her, she awakens, and after a violent scene of charges on his part and denial on hers, he smothers her. Emilia comes in. She says Cassio has killed Roderigo. Desdemona's dying voice is heard; Othello owns to the murder, and Emilia's cries bring in Cassio, Iago, and others. As Iago confirms Othello's story of Desdemona's unfaithfulness, Emilia tells the truth about the handkerchief. Iago sees that all deception is at an end and hurries away; some attendants follow to arrest him. Meanwhile Othello drops his sword, and, apparently unarmed, goes towards the bed, then, suddenly drawing forth a dagger, kills himself as the curtain falls.

RIGOLETTO.*

RIGOLETTO, the hero of this opera, is jester to and general pamperer of the licentious tastes of his master, the Duke of Mantua. His body, like his mind, is loathsome, being crooked and hump-backed. Through his connivance the domestic peace of two noblemen of the court has

---

* First performed at Venice in March, 1851 ; and at Covent Garden, May 14th, 1853. Mme. Melba made her operatic début in this opera at Brussels, Oct. 12th, 1887.

been broken in upon, *i.e.*, the Count Ceprane and the Count Monterone. The former determines to have his revenge on the servant, Rigoletto, while the latter openly accuses the master, the Duke, of seducing his daughter, and, being led off to prison, calls down the vengeance of heaven on both. Rigoletto is terribly impressed with this curse, and retires to seek comfort from the only pure thing connected with him, and that is his daughter Gilda. This maiden he keeps closely confined, only allowing her to go out once a week to church, and of whose existence, as his daughter, no one has any idea. The Duke, ever on the look out for a pretty face, has nevertheless marked her at her devotions, and, in the garb of a student, he manages to declare to her his pretended love. Meanwhile, Count Ceprano has found out that Rigoletto pays visits to the house where his daughter is confined, and, it being next door to his own, determines upon a plot to outdo the hump-backed jester. He gets a band of his followers to pretend that they are about to abduct his wife, the Countess Ceprano, and by that means secure the assistance of Rigoletto, who, blindfolded, holds the ladder while they really seize upon his daughter and hand her over to the tender mercies of the Duke. They having secured their prize and gone, Rigoletto takes off the bandage, only to find that he has assisted in the dishonour of his own child. Mad with rage and shame he swoons, and with this ends Act I.

Rigoletto then hires an assassin called Sparafucile to kill the Duke, and his sister Magdalena allures the Duke into a secluded public-house to assist her brother in his work of blood; but, being charmed with his manners, she determines, if possible, to effect his escape. Meantime, Rigoletto, having ordered Gilda to put on male attire preparatory to her departure for Verona, leads her to the house in which the Duke is making himself very pleasant to Magdalena, in order to show her how faithless her lover is: for, in spite of the dishonour he has brought upon her, she cannot help loving him. While outside she hears Sparafucile and his sister talking, the latter pleading for the Duke's life, and the former declaring that he must either kill him or a substitute. Gilda, with a devotion worthy of a better cause, determines to sacrifice her life, and, entering the house, is stabbed to the heart by Sparafucile, and her body is put in a sack to be handed over to Rigoletto as the dead Duke. Rigoletto returns to inquire how matters have gone, and, on paying the arranged sum of money, the sack is given to him. He is exulting over the death of his master and the seducer of his daughter, when he hears the Duke's voice from behind. His suspicions are aroused, and, opening the sack, he discovers, to his horror, his dying daughter. In despair he falls at her side, and on this scene the curtain drops.

LA TRAVIATA.*

THE scene of this opera is laid in and about Paris at the commencement of the eighteenth century.

Alfred Germont, son of Signor George Germont, becomes deeply enamoured of Violetta Valery, a lady of light character, and she, though at first laughing at the idea, at length returns his love, and, leaving her dissolute life and companions, retires into the country with him. Signor Germont, anxious for his son's welfare, there finds her, and, in the absence of her lover, so works upon her feelings that she promises to break with him. She does this by accepting an invitation to a ball given by one of her old companions, Flora Eervois, and goes there under the protection of Baron Douphol. Alfred Germont hearing of this meets them there, and a most heartrending scene takes place, when he before all declares her faithless, and in his frenzy behaves in a most ungallant manner.

Violetta, heartbroken, disgraced, and dying, is discovered in the last scene in her bedroom. Signor Germont having told his son that Violetta only left him at his own urgent request, they are both so struck with remorse that they come, the one to accept her as his daughter, and the other to claim her as his bride ; but they are too late, and only get there in time to be forgiven by the dying and injured woman, and to make the last moments of the poor creature happy by their presence.

IL TROVATORE.†

THE first scene opens in a passage in the Palace of Aliaferia, where the Count de Luna has apartments. Here one of his servants tells a piece of the family history to his comrades. How the Count de Luna had two sons, the younger one of whom was "spoken over" by a gipsy when a child. The woman was burnt, but the child disappeared, and was supposed to have been stolen and killed by the gipsy's daughter.

The next scene discovers Leonora in the palace gardens. She is one of the Queen's attendants. She tells her friend who is with her how she loves

---

* Was produced at Venice in March, 1853 ; and in London at Her Majesty's Theatre, May 24th, 1856. The opera was written in a month.

Christine Nilsson made her *début* as Violetta in this opera at the Théâtre Lyrique, Paris, on Oct. 27th, 1864; and at Her Majesty's Theatre, London, in 1867, in the same part.

† Was produced at Rome in January, 1853 ; and at Covent Garden, May 17th, 1855.

the Troubadour Manrico, whom she first met at the tournament, when as an unknown warrior he won the day. They go into the palace, while the Count de Luna enters the garden. He sees a light in Leonora's window. He is desperately in love with her, and is about to rush up to her room, when he hears the lute of the Troubadour in the garden, and conceals himself. Leonora comes out to meet her lover, and at first mistakes the Count for him. Manrico approaches, and then Leonora, to the great rage of the Count, declares Manrico to be the man she loves, The rivals quarrel and retire to fight a duel, and so ends the first Act.

The second Act discloses a ruined house in Brittany, the home of the gipsies. Azucena, the daughter of the witch burnt by the Count de Luna, is there, and so is Manrico, who is her reputed son, but in reality the son of the Count de Luna, and brother of the present Count. Day is breaking, and Azucena recounts to the gipsies round the fire how, when her mother was burned, she threw her own son, by mistake for Manrico, into the fire that was consuming her mother. She reproaches Manrico for having spared De Luna's life when it was in his power in the duel. A messenger enters with a letter for Manrico. He is chosen by the Prince to defend Castellor, and is told further that Leonora, thinking him dead, is going to enter a convent that night. He leaves the gipsy camp.

In the next scene the Count de Luna, thinking his rival is dead (for Manrico has been severely wounded in battle lately by De Luna's followers), approaches the convent to seize Leonora on her way to the altar. A chorus of nuns is heard within the walls, and Leonora comes with her lady friends to take the veil. As she is bidding them farewell the Count seizes her, but Manrico appears like a ghost. Manrico's followers appear and take the Count prisoner. Leonora goes with Manrico.

In the third Act the Count de Luna is storming Castellor. Azucena, who has followed Manrico, is brought prisoner into his camp. He finds out she is Manrico's reputed mother, and daughter of the gipsy who burned (as he thinks) his young brother, and he orders her to be burnt. Manrico is in the citadel, and is on the point of entering the chapel to marry Leonora, when the news is brought him of Azucena's position. He rushes to her rescue.

In the last Act Leonora approaches the prison window of Manrico, who is confined in the palace of Aliaferia with the gipsy Azucena. The Count has ordered his execution for the next day, and that Azucena should be burnt. Leonora meets the Count and intercedes for Manrico, and even goes the length of promising to become the Count's wife if he will spare Manrico. He consents, but Leonora takes the poison from a ring she wears, determined never to become the Count's wife. She goes to Manrico's prison. She tells him the price she is paying for his liberty in accepting De Luna, and implores him to be gone. He curses her for her want of fidelity to him, not knowing that she is only waiting for the poison to take effect. She falls to the ground, and then tells him all. The Count enters to witness her death, and delivers Manrico to his soldiers for execution. He turns to Azucena and points to the execution of her son from the window, when, to his horror, he hears from her that he has killed his own brother. Azucena falls dead, having avenged her mother, and the Count is left alone, " doomed to live."

WAGNER.

RICHARD WAGNER, the greatest of all composers for the stage, was born at Leipsic on May 22nd, 1813. He was educated at Dresden and in the university of his native town. At an early age he was made Musical Director of the Theatre Royal, Dresden, where his operas "Rienzi," "Der Fliegende Holländer," and "Tannhäuser" were first performed. In the year 1848, being involved in political troubles, he took refuge in Zurich. In 1855 he directed the Philharmonic Society Concerts in London. On May 22nd, 1872, Wagner laid the foundation stone of a theatre at Bayreuth, which was opened in the year 1876 with the first complete performance of the trilogy, "Der Ring des Nibelungen." The first performance of his last opera, "Parsifal," took place there in July, 1882. He died at Venice, Feb. 13th, 1883.

DER FLIEGENDE HOLLÄNDER.*

THE opening scene represents a gulf surrounded by rocks. A Norwegian ship lies at anchor—there is a storm raging. Daland, captain of the vessel, descends from the rocks and describes how, having been driven before the storm, he has been forced to seek shelter in this bay, his own home being but a few miles up the coast. Having given orders to keep a sharp look-out, he goes below, leaving the helmsman on deck, who, singing a song about his love on shore, gradually falls asleep. The storm increases, and suddenly in the far distance the phantom ship appears bearing down rapidly for the bay. It runs in alongside the Norwegian vessel and casts anchor. The crew of the phantom ship then silently furl sail, and the Flying Dutchman, captain of the vessel, attired in black, steps on shore. He tells his tale of woe; how he is doomed to traverse the seas for seven years at a time, when he may land and try to break the curse, but failing, he has again to start for a like period. How in storm and battle he has sought and prayed for death, but to no purpose. Daland comes on deck, and, seeing the

* First performed at Dresden, Jan. 2nd, 1843 ; in London, July 23rd, 1870. The idea of writing an opera on this subject occurred to the composer while going by sea from Riga to London on his way to Paris—a long and stormy voyage.

strange vessel alongside, after waking the helmsman, calls on the Dutchman to declare himself. He tells him his nationality, and craves him to give him lodging in his house, offering in return great treasures. At a sign, two of the Dutch sailors convey a chest on shore full of pearls and precious stones, which so delight the avaricious Daland that he further promises, on the Dutchman asking him, to give him his daughter Senta's hand in marriage. While they are talking the storm abates, and the first Acts ends with both vessels preparing to put to sea to make for the port where Daland lives.

The scene of the next Act is a room in Daland's house. Dame Mary and maidens are discovered spinning and singing. Senta, Daland's daughter, is sitting apart gazing at a portrait of the Flying Dutchman which hangs on the wall. Her companions laugh at her for being so much engrossed with the portrait. She declares that could she but meet him she would break the curse under which he exists, and then sings the ballad of "The Flying Dutchman," telling how, when nearing a cape in a storm, he called upon the foul fiend himself to stop him from rounding the point, and that for this blasphemy he is compelled to roam the seas until he finds some maiden who will consent to marry him; how every seven years he is permitted to land to try and find the woman who will thus devote herself to him; and she finishes by wildly declaring that she shall do so. At this moment Erik, her lover, enters, who, having overheard her declaration, prays her not to forsake him. He then tells her that he is fearful, having had a strange and vivid dream, and describes how he saw Daland meet with the Flying Dutchman on the coast during a storm, and that bringing him home, she, Senta, rushed out to greet them, and fell on her knees at the feet of the accursed one; how he raised her up and pressed her to his heart; that she left with him, and both disappeared flying o'er the main. On his finishing she again wildly declares she will save him, and Erik, shocked, rushes from her presence. Hardly has he gone when Daland and the Dutchman enter. Her father tells her to give the stranger a kind reception, as he is her affianced husband, and leaves them; she, comparing him with the portrait, sees her lover's dream fulfilled, and on the Dutchman asking her to wed him, consents.

The last Act opens with the bay outside Daland's house, by night; his vessel and the phantom ship are at anchor. The Norwegian vessel is lighted up and the crew are making merry, while the Dutchman is as dark and silent as night itself. Girls enter bearing baskets of provisions, and they and the Norwegian sailors call on the Dutch crew to wake up and join them in their carousals. Suddenly a slight movement is noticeable on board the phantom vessel, and a melancholy light is hoisted to the mast head, and while the Dutch crew break into a wild

and mysterious chorus, calling on their captain to return, the sea around
the vessel rolls and tosses, and the wind is heard whistling through the
rigging, while the rest of the bay is calm. The Norwegians try to sing
the Dutchmen down, but, getting frightened, at length run away. The
Dutch crew then cease, and all is silent again. The door of Daland's
house opens and Senta rushes out, followed by Erik, begging her to
remember her old vows to him, describing how she promised to be
his bride. The Flying Dutchman, who, unseen, has overheard them,
steps forward, and, proclaiming her a traitress, bids her farewell. She
prays him to stop, declaring she knows who he is. He tells her she
cannot, and then, proclaiming himself to be the Flying Dutchman,
steps on board and sails from shore. Senta, breaking away from her
companions and Erik, who are trying to restrain her, rushes up one of
the rocks, and declaring herself to be faithful to him with her last breath,
throws herself into the sea. The phantom ship out at sea is seen
suddenly to founder, and the Dutchman and Senta are then descried
rising from the waves clasped in one another's arms.

LOHENGRIN.[*]

THE scene opens on the banks of the Scheldt, near Antwerp. Henry
I., King of Germany, has come to Antwerp to levy forces against the
Hungarians, but finds discord and disorder rife in Antwerp, and calls
upon Frederick of Telramund to explain the cause of it. Frederick
relates how he is the guardian of the late Duke of Brabant's two children,
Godfrey and Elsa, but that Godfrey has been murdered by his sister Elsa,
leaving him (Frederick) heir to the dukedom. The King calls upon Elsa
to prove her innocence. A trial by combat is to take place. On the one
side is Frederick, to prove his accusation. No one appears as Elsa's
champion. She dreamily sings of a glittering knight who will come to
help her, and at last, after several summonses by trumpet, a boat drawn
by a swan glides down the river. In the boat stands Lohengrin, Knight
of the Holy Grail, who steps ashore and undertakes to fight for Elsa if
she will consent to be his wife ; but he adds the condition that she is
never to ask who he is in rank or by name. She consents to his terms.
The combat takes place, and Frederick is defeated, though Lohengrin
spares his life.

The second Act opens with a scene between Frederick and his wife,
Ortrud, daughter of the Prince of Friesland. Frederick reproaches her

---

[*] First performed under Liszt at Weimar, August, 1850 ; in London, May, 1875.

with having caused his disgrace by telling him falsely to accuse Elsa. Ortrud informs him that Lohengrin will lose his power if Elsa can be induced to get him to disclose his name. They determine upon doing this. It is night, and they are on the steps of the minster. Elsa appears in the balcony of the palace opposite to them, sees Ortrud, and, pitying her loneliness and exclusion from the palace festivities, invites her into the Kemenate, or abode of the women. The day breaks. The nobles of Brabant assemble on the minster steps and greet each other. Heralds proclaim Frederick as outlawed; the stranger knight, Lohengrin, as the guardian of Brabant. Elsa approaches the minster in bridal procession. Ortrud is with her. Suddenly Ortrud bars her way to the church, taunts her with not knowing her husband's name, and insists upon having precedence in the procession. The King and Lohengrin, however, arrive, and lead Elsa in, but not before Frederick has stepped from behind a buttress, and, in a whispered conversation, has told her that he can help her to ensure for herself everlasting faithfulness in her husband and a knowledge of all his secrets. The curtain falls as she enters the cathedral.

In the third Act Lohengrin and Elsa are conducted to the bridal-chamber, where the King and nobles leave them. After a beautiful love duet, she breaks her vow, and asks him who he is. At this moment Frederick and four Brabant nobles burst into the room with drawn swords. Lohengrin seizes his and strikes Frederick lifeless. The nobles kneel to him and then remove Frederick's dead body.

In the last scene the King and nobles are assembled on the banks of the stream. Lohengrin has promised to reveal his name and condition to Elsa, and she comes to hear it. He tells them all how he is Lohengrin, son of the great Percival, who guards the cup of the Holy Grail on Mount Salvat, and how he was sent to Antwerp as Knight of the Holy Grail to fight Elsa's battle. The swan appears again on the stream. Lohengrin tells them the Grail has sent for him. He gives Elsa his sword, a ring, and his horn for her brother, who he prophesies will return alive to her. Ortrud steps forward exultingly, tells Elsa how the swan is her brother Godfrey—whom she herself by magic thus transformed—and taunts her with the fact that her own brother is taking Lohengrin from her. Lohengrin prays: the dove of the Holy Grail descends. Lohengrin removes the gold chain from the swan's neck, and restores Godfrey to his sister. He himself steps into the boat, which is drawn away by the dove, while Godfrey is proclaimed Duke of Brabant, and Elsa is overcome with grief at Lohengrin's departure.

In the opera, Lohengrin, Knight of the Holy Grail, is introduced as a symbol of Christianity, defeating Frieslandish heathenism in the wiles and machinations of the sorceress Ortrud.

DIE MEISTERSINGER VON NUREMBURG.*

THE action of this opera takes place in Nuremburg in the middle of the sixteenth century. As the curtain rises on Act I., a section of St. Katharine's Church is seen, showing the last rows of seats. The service is just ending. Sir Walther von Stolzing, a young knight, stands gazing at Eva, the daughter of Pognor, a goldsmith, and Mastersinger, who with Magdalena, her nurse, are concluding their devotions. As the congregation pass out he presses towards her, asking her if she is betrothed; he is told that her hand is to be given to the winner of the Meistersinger's prize on the following St. John's Day. David, an apprentice to Hans Sachs, a cobbler (and who, by the way, is in love with Magdalena), enters, and explains how a preliminary trial for the Meister's prize is to be held directly on that very spot. As the two girls go out, Walther passionately expresses his determination to enter the lists and carry Eva off as prize. Apprentices enter and arrange seats and the curtained box for the marker (the judge of the singing), while David expounds to Walther the difficulties attending a candidate for the honour of Mastersinger. The apprentices, having erected the marker's box wrongly, are corrected by David; it is put right as Pognor and Beckmesser, the town clerk, enter. Beckmesser is in hopes that Pognor will agree to his wooing his daughter Eva. Walther steps forward asking for admittance into the guild of Meistersingers: he is introduced to the other Meistersingers, who now assemble. Pognor announces that on the morrow the prize is to be his daughter. Walther is accepted as a candidate, and after having sung of how he learnt his art from nature, Beckmesser enters the marker's box, and the young knight begins his trial song. Loud scratchings of chalk on a slate come from the box, indicating Beckmesser's disapproval. Confusion and disagreement quickly arise, only Sachs finding truth and beauty in the attempt, and asking for no hasty judgment; but the meeting soon breaks up in disorder, Walther angry and discouraged as the curtain falls.

The scene of the second Act is a street: Sachs' house in one corner, Pognor's house opposite. As the curtain rises David is fastening his master's shutters, and the apprentices are similarly engaged on other houses. Magdalena comes out and David tells her that Walther has been defeated on his trial song. The apprentices chaff David about Magdalena: as David is about to rush at them Sachs enters; they all disperse, and the cobbler leads David into his house. Pognor and Eva

---

* First performed at Munich, June 21st, 1868; and in London, at the Drury Lane Theatre, under Richter, May 30th, 1882.

return from a walk ; they seat themselves under a linden tree. Magdalena appears; in an aside she tells Eva of Walther's failure. They go into the house as Sachs appears with work-bench and stool, which are placed outside Sachs' door. The cobbler muses to himself in between his work ; he is haunted by Walther's song, seeing much beauty in its newness. Eva comes out and crosses over; she learns from Sachs of the disagreement over Walther's singing, and is cross because he does not say he will befriend him. Magdalena appears urging Eva to return home, and says that Beckmesser is coming that evening to serenade her. It is arranged that Magdalena should take Eva's place at the window so that David should be made jealous. Walther enters, Magdalena quickly going into the house, warning Eva not to remain out long. In the short duet that follows between the lovers, Walther declares his incapability of winning the prize, and urges Eva to fly with him. The watchman's horn is heard; Magdalena calls Eva within. The watchman passes, calling out it is ten o'clock and that lights must be put out. Eva again appears, now in Magdalena's dress. As she and Walther are preparing to run off down a side street, Sachs, who has heard their plan from his doorway, suddenly turns round the light at which he has been working in such a way that they are illuminated. At this moment, too, Beckmesser enters with his lute to serenade Eva, and the lovers conceal themselves beneath the foliage of the linden tree. As the town clerk is about to begin his serenade, Sachs suddenly hammers loudly on his last and sings himself noisily. Beckmesser is naturally annoyed. Finally an agreement is made that Sachs is to act as "marker," Beckmesser pretending he is trying his song for the morrow. Every error is recorded by Sachs with a loud hit of his hammer on the last. The confusion increases. David pops his head out and sees Beckmesser serenading, as he perceives, with sharper eyes than the latter, no other than Magdalena. Meistersingers and others, some in night-dress, apprentices, gradually fill the stage as Beckmesser comes in for a sound beating from the jealous David. The row is only quelled by the sound of the watchman's horn, and as all disperse, Sachs kicks David into his house, pushes Eva up her father's steps, and drags Walther in with him, thus preventing a second attempt at flight on the part of the lovers. No one is left on the stage as the watchman again crosses, calling out the hour. The full moon shines out, illuminating the empty scene, as the curtain falls.

The third Act is in two scenes, the first of which is the interior of Sachs' workshop. Sachs is discovered absorbed in a book. David enters and asks forgiveness for the previous evening's folly, and presently goes out, after having sung his lesson-song, a little chorale in honour of his master's birthday (he is learning the art from him as well as cobbling), and Sachs is left alone. The master cobbler moralizes on the folly of mankind, and presently Walther comes in from an inner chamber. He has had a beautiful dream, which Sachs makes him describe in song, taking down the words. Two verses of the prize song are thus composed, and the pair leave the room to array themselves in festival dress. Enter Beckmesser from the street, dressed in his best, but in a miserable condition; he limps about the room in agitated remembrance of the previous evening. Suddenly he catches sight of the manuscript of Walther's song. Thinking it to be a trial-song of Sachs, he quickly hides it in his pocket as Sachs appears at the chamber door. It appears to him that Sachs is bent on winning Eva himself; this makes him furiously jealous, and eventually when, naturally, Sachs denies it, he produces the paper as proof. Sachs says quietly he may keep it. At first suspicious of some further trickery, as he thinks, Beckmesser is at length enraptured, going off intending to use the verses himself. Eva now comes into the shop pretending that something is amiss with her shoe. As Sachs attends to it, Walther appears in his festival dress, and, with eyes fixed on Eva, sings the third verse of the prize song. David and Magdalena enter also, gaily dressed, and the scene ends with the famous quintet. The curtain rises for the last time, showing an open meadow near the town. The stage is crowded with merry-makers; bands of cobblers, town watchmen, journeymen, tailors, &c., march in procession; a dance follows; and finally the Meistersingers themselves take their places on a raised daïs. Beckmesser now attempts to sing, fitting the words of Walther's song to his own serenade with such a foolish result that he is hooted. It is Walther's turn. The dream song captivates all, and Eva places the laurel wreath on his brow; but he refuses the Meistersingers' gold chain from Pognor as typical of their pedantry, until Sachs points out to him what the true value of learning really is.

DER RING DES NIBELUNGEN.

THIS magnificent series of four operas was first performed in its entirety at Bayreuth in 1876, and in London at Her Majesty's Theatre in May, 1882. The whole work is far too elaborate to be properly explained in this small book; there are, however, plenty of handbooks to be had which may be conveniently studied with the librettos. Here we shall only give a brief outline of each opera in the proper order of performance.

DAS RHEINGOLD.*

THIS, the prelude to the trilogy, is in four scenes, played without break. The first shows us the bottom of the Rhine. The three Rhine-maidens are swimming to and fro guarding the Rhine-gold. Alberich, chief of the Nibelungen dwarfs, succeeds in stealing it from them, but only by a renunciation of love. The scene changes to an open space, with the castle of Walhalla shining in the background. The god Wotan hails the at length completed structure. It has been built by the giants Fasolt and Fafner. As payment, Freia, the goddess of the love-apples which give eternal youth, has been promised by Wotan. Freia enters, and the giants follow to take her as agreed; but Wotan refuses, and asks them to accept other reward. Froh, the rainbow-god, and Donner, the god of thunder, come in to protect her, and presently Loge, the fire-god. The last explains how he has been travelling far and wide to find a substitute for Freia, but has not succeeded—nothing can equal the worth of woman; but he has learnt that Alberich has renounced love in acquiring the Rhine-gold, from which he has fashioned an all-powerful ring. The giants say that they will give up Freia if Wotan will secure them the Rhine-gold. They then go off, taking the goddess with them as pledge. Immediately a pale mist fills the stage, the gods seeming to take on an aged and withered look. Loge explains the reason: Freia, the goddess of the apples of eternal youth, has gone. Wotan thereupon determines on taking possession of the Rhine-gold. He and Loge disappear in a cleft in the rocks, and the scene changes to the cavern of the Nibelungs. Alberich drags in Mime, his brother, who lets fall the "Tarnhelm" (invisible cap), which he has just made. Alberich places it on his head, and immediately disappears. Wotan and Loge enter. Mime tells them what a hard taskmaster Alberich is now that he has made the ring from the Rhine-gold. Alberich appears, driving before him a band of Nibelungs carrying gold and silver jewellery, which they place in a pile on the stage, and are then driven off. Alberich tells Wotan that he has the gods now in his power. Loge asks to be shown the power of this wonderful "Tarnhelm," so Alberich puts it on and assumes the shape of a monster serpent. On his re-appearance Loge asks whether he cannot turn himself into something smaller. Alberich immediately turns himself into a toad. Wotan puts his foot on it, Loge seizes the "Tarnhelm," and Alberich is seen writhing in his own shape. He is bound hand and foot with a rope and dragged off. The scene changes back to the open space of the second scene. Alberich is bidden to call up the treasure.

---

* First performed at Munich, Sept. 22nd 1869 ; in London, at Her Majesty's, May, 1812 ; in English, at Covent Garden, Jan. 27th, 1908.

He puts the ring to his lips and mutters a secret spell. The Nibelungs appear bringing the gold and silver hoard. Wotan then seizes the ring from Alberich and places it on his finger. Alberich is set free; he goes off, but before doing so utters a terrible curse upon the ring, that it shall never bring happiness to its possessor. Fricka, Donner, and Froh enter, and after them the giants and Freia. The giants thrust their staves into the ground and Freia is placed behind, and the golden treasure is piled up to completely conceal her. There is not sufficient, so the "Tarnhelm" has to be added. Still the giants detect a tiny opening: the ring must be given up, too. Wotan refuses, but Erda, the earth-goddess, suddenly appears and warns Wotan that he must give way. The ring is accordingly added to the pile, the giants are satisfied, Freia is released. On taking off the treasure the giants begin quarrelling, and Fafner, raising his staff, fells Fasolt to the ground. Thus does the curse of Alberich begin to work. The opera ends with a procession of the gods over the rainbow bridge. to Walhalla. The voices of the Rhine-maidens are heard in the distance bemoaning the theft of the Rhine-gold.

DIE WALKÜRE.*

THE scene of the first Act is the interior of the dwelling of Hunding, built round a huge ash tree. A violent storm is just subsiding as the door at the back opens and Siegmund enters. He throws himself down exhausted before the fire. Sieglinde, Hunding's wife, comes in from an inner room; she sees the stranger, and at his request brings him water, and, later, a horn of mead. Refreshed, he is prepared to leave, but Sieglinde asks him to await Hunding's return. Hunding enters; the three take their places at the table, and during the evening meal Siegmund relates his adventures: that he is the son of Wolfing; that on returning from a hunt one day he found his home laid waste and his twin sister gone; further, that lately, in attempting to rescue a woman in distress, he lost his weapons. Hunding discovers in Siegmund a mortal foe, but offers his hospitality for the night, saying they must meet and fight on the morrow. Hunding and Sieglinde leave him alone. His musings by the fire are interrupted by the entrance of Sieglinde once more; she has given her husband a sleeping draught, and urges Siegmund to flee. She relates how at her marriage feast a mysterious man had entered and had driven a sword up to the hilt in the ash tree's stem.

* First performed at Munich, June 25th, 1870; in London, at Her Majesty's, May, 1882; in English, at Covent Garden, Oct. 16th, 1895.

No one could draw it forth and claim it as prize. But meanwhile, in the earlier scene, the pair had discovered their mutual attraction for one another. Sieglinde says that he, Siegmund, is the hero for whom the sword was intended. The ensuing love duet is interrupted by Siegmund drawing the sword in triumph from the tree. The pair realize that they are twin brother and sister, and the curtain falls on their departure into the forest.

The scene of the second Act is a wild, rocky pass among the mountains. Wotan directs Brünnhilde, the Valkyrie, to support Siegmund in his fight with Hunding, but Fricka enters and eventually succeeds in persuading Wotan to withdraw the protection in the interests of the sanctity of the marriage tie. Brünnhilde returns, and Wotan explains his despair; that the sword has been won by Siegmund, as he had intended, but that now the latter must pay the penalty. If so his plans for recovering the ring and treasure from Fafner must fail, at any moment Alberich may succeed, and then the gods are certainly doomed. Reluctantly Brünnhilde agrees not to protect Siegmund, and Wotan goes off. Brünnhilde sees Sieglinde and Siegmund approaching, and goes out of sight, into a cave. Sieglinde is exhausted with her flight and soon sinks into a swoon. Brünnhilde advances towards Siegmund and tells him that he must prepare for the joys of Walhalla. He refuses to leave Sieglinde. She says his sword's virtue will no longer be of avail in the coming fight, but eventually, after his passionate pleading, she is so touched by his love for the woman that she agrees to disobey Wotan and help him. Darkness comes on apace. Hunding appears, and the fight takes place. Brünnhilde duly attempts to protect Siegmund, but Wotan is there, and Hunding is victorious. Brünnhilde hastily picks up Siegmund's broken sword and hurries away with Sieglinde. Wotan, after a contemptuous "Go!" to Hunding, who thereupon falls dead, goes off to punish Brünnhilde for her disobedience.

The third Act shows us the punishment of Brünnhilde. The scene is the summit of a rocky mountain. The eight Valkyries, the war-maidens, are assembled. To them enters Brünnhilde with Sieglinde. Brünnhilde asks each Valkyrie in turn to lend her a horse to effect Sieglinde's escape, but the Valkyries are afraid of Wotan's anger, and refuse. Brünnhilde gives Siegmund's broken sword to Sieglinde, telling her to keep it for her unborn son, Siegfried, that she must fly by herself, and that she, Brünnhilde, will stay and await Wotan's wrath. Sieglinde hurries away. Presently Wotan appears in a terrible rage. The eight Valkyries surrounding Brünnhilde endeavour to pacify him, but he warns them not to fall foul of his wrath as well. They go off quickly, and Wotan and Brünnhilde are left alone. In this final scene Brünnhilde insists that in disobeying Wotan she had only carried out his secret wishes, and at length her sentence is mitigated. She is, indeed, to lose her divinity, but the man who is to awaken her from the deep sleep into which she is to be cast shall, at any rate, be hero enough to surmount the ring of magic fire that will be set round her couch. The curtain falls upon Brünnhilde lying under a fir tree and Wotan slowly disappearing through the circle of fire.

SIEGFRIED.*

THE first Act of "Siegfried" is laid in the cave where Mime has brought up Siegfried. His mother, Sieglinde, died in giving birth to Siegmund's son, and the dwarf has taken over the boy, hoping that he may in manhood slay Fafner and win for him the Nibelung treasure, which Fafner, who has turned himself into a dragon, the better to guard it, hoards in a cave in the forest near by. As the curtain rises Mime is engaged in making a sword for Siegfried, complaining that he has never made one yet that the boy does not break. Siegfried enters, snaps the new sword in pieces, and rates Mime for his incompetence. He then compels the dwarf to tell him the truth of his parentage, saying that he has discovered in nature that children are like their parents, so that Mime's pretence of being his father is patently absurd. The dwarf then tells him how Sieglinde died in giving him birth, and produces the fragments of Siegmund's sword as proof of his story. Siegfried immediately orders Mime to forge the sword anew, and runs off into the wood. Mime returns to the anvil in great trouble, because he knows he cannot repair the sword. Just at this moment Wotan appears, disguised as a Wanderer. There ensues a scene between the two, in which the Wanderer stakes his head against that of the dwarf in a contest of wits. Mime accordingly asks three questions: who are the race who dwell in the bowels of the earth? who sojourn on the earth's back? and who dwell in the welkin above? The Wanderer answers each question, the Nibelungs, the giants, and the Aesir; and then asks three questions himself: what was the race that Wotan ruthlessly dealt with and yet held most dear? Mime answers, the Volsungs, and is also able to answer the question, with what sword shall Siegfried slay the dragon? "Nothung," that is, Siegmund's broken weapon. But when the Wanderer asks him who shall forge it, Mime cannot answer. The Wanderer tells him, he only who doesn't know what fear is, and goes off, adding that he leaves his forfeited head to the fearless hero. Siegfried re-enters and asks for the sword; Mime, mindful of the Wanderer's parting words, realizes that he has never taught Siegfried what fear is. He tries to

---

* First performed at Bayreuth in 1876 ; in London in 1882 ; in English in 1901.

make him understand, and fails, and then he tells Siegfried to forge the sword for himself, and while this is being done, sets to work himself in making a poisoned draught, which he will offer to Siegfried after he has fought and killed the dragon. The curtain descends upon Siegfried splitting the anvil in twain with the newly forged blade.

The scene of the second Act is a glade in the forest, with Fafner's cave at the back. It is night. Alberich is brooding gloomily over the vain hope of recovering the treasure. The Wanderer comes in and tells him that Mime and Siegfried are near at hand, that he himself will stand aside, and that Alberich and Mime can settle the matter of the treasure for themselves. He then wakens Fafner, whom Alberich warns of approaching danger, asking for the ring, that he may then help to protect him and to keep his treasure in peace. Fafner's voice is heard saying he is in possession, and intends to remain so. The Wanderer laughs and goes off, and presently Alberich slinks away, as dawn breaks and Siegfried and Mime come in. The latter tries again to awaken fear in Siegfried by describing the dragon, but Siegfried laughs and tells him to leave him; he will await the dragon's appearance and stick "Nothung" into his vitals. Siegfried reclines under a tree and recalls his childhood and the story of his mother's death. Presently he hears a bird singing. He cuts a pipe from a rush, but failing to make it sound, blows merrily on his horn. The sound awakens Fafner, who comes out of his cave, Siegfried rushes at him with the sword and slays him. On drawing out the weapon his hand comes in contact with the dragon's blood, which he involuntarily puts to his lips. The power of understanding the song of birds is immediately his, and the bird is heard telling him of the ring and treasure lying in the cave. Into this he disappears, as Alberich from one side of the stage and Mime from the other meet for a moment in an angry scene, Alberich refusing to share the treasure with his brother. For the present, though, it belongs to Siegfried, who now comes out of the cave. He puts the " Tarnhelm " in his girdle and the ring on his finger, as the dwarfs slip out of sight. Again the bird sings, and tells him to beware of Mime. Mime enters and offers the poisoned draught. His plausible words have no effect on Siegfried, who is able now, through the power of the dragon's blood, to read the true meaning of the dwarf's advances. In a sudden impulse of disgust he deals a swift blow at Mime, who falls dead, while Alberich's mocking laughter is heard from the side. Once more the bird is heard singing, telling the young hero of the glorious wife awaiting him on the fire-girt rock, and the curtain falls on Siegfried hurrying off, following the bird, to awaken her.

The first scene of the third Act shows a wild region at the foot of a rocky mountain. Night. The Wanderer enters and calls upon Erda, who appears in a chasm in the rocks. He asks her to say what the future has in store for the gods. She cannot tell him. He bursts forth into a magnificent declaration of his fearing not the Aesir's ending, since it but works his will; that Siegfried, all undirected, has achieved the ring, will overcome Alberich's curse, and awaken Brünnhilde. Erda disappears, and Siegfried comes in, following the bird. The Wanderer arrests his progress, as though to test for himself the young hero's fearlessness and power. At the end of the colloquy he bars the way up the mountain with his spear. Siegfried strikes it with his sword and the spear breaks; and as the Wanderer quickly hastens away, Siegfried is seen climbing up the side of the mountain, now alive with flickering flames. The scene changes to that of the third Act of "The Valkyrie." Brünnhilde lies asleep, and as the flames die down, Siegfried appears. He awakens her with a kiss, and there ensues a duet, during which Brünnhilde has first to reconcile herself to her loss of divinity before she can accept the love Siegfried so passionately tenders.

DIE GÖTTERDÄMMERUNG.*

THE opera begins with a prologue, the scene of which is the same as the final scene in "Siegfried." It is night, and as the curtain rises the three Norns are dimly seen. They describe how, now that Wotan's all-powerful spear is broken, the god awaits the end; that Walhalla is ranged round with faggots ready for the final conflagration soon to come, but when they cannot say. The golden rope of divination snaps, and, binding themselves together with the pieces, they disappear. Morning dawns, and Brünnhilde and Siegfried appear. Brünnhilde gives the hero her horse, and he to her the ring, as a pledge of his love and constancy. He goes off in search of fresh adventure, and the scene changes, without break in the music, to that of the first Act. As the curtains open again the hall of the Gibichungs, overlooking the Rhine, is disclosed. Gunther and his sister Gutrune and Hagen are in conversation. The latter character is the son of Alberich. He knows the story of the ring, that Siegfried now possesses it, and proposes a plan for getting the hero into his power. Gunther is unmarried; it is suggested to him that he should woo Brünnhilde. As none but the greatest of heroes can ever surmount the fire-girt rock, Hagen says that Siegfried should bring her to Gunther, and that by giving him a magic draught he could be made to forget her completely, and to succumb to the charms of Gutrune. Siegfried's horn-call is heard, and presently the hero arrives. Gutrune offers him the draught as arranged, and he is immediately attracted by her. He soon

---

* First performed at Bayreuth, 1876; in London, May, 1882; in English, at Covent Garden, Feb. 1st, 1908.

declares that if Gunther will give him his sister for wife he will in return bring to him Brünnhilde. It is agreed, and after swearing friendship, Siegfried and Gunther depart for the Valkyrie's rock. Hagen is left alone. He has a short soliloquy expressing his satisfaction at the progress of his plan for capturing the all-powerful ring. The scene changes back to that of the prologue. To Brünnhilde there enters Waltraute, who comes to implore her to give back the ring to the Rhine-maidens; that that alone can save the gods from destruction, who even now are awaiting the end in Walhalla. Brünnhilde asks how can she give up the pledge of Siegfried's love, and Waltraute goes away in despair. With the aid of the "Tarnhelm," Siegfried now appears in the guise of Gunther, and, after a desperate struggle tears the ring from Brünnhilde's finger, bids her enter the cave, and follows, first drawing his sword and swearing fidelity to his new friend.

The scene of the second Act is the exterior of the Gibichungs' hall. As the curtain rises Hagen is seen sitting asleep against a pillar of the hall. Alberich is crouching near, and urges his son to exert all his powers to obtain the ring. Dawn comes. Alberich disappears, and Siegfried enters to say that Gunther and Brünnhilde are following. Gutrune comes out of the hall, and Siegfried tells her that although he brought Brünnhilde from the fire mountain, his sword is a witness to his fidelity to both her and her brother. The two go into the hall, and Hagen summons the vassals to the forthcoming marriage festivities. Gunther and Brünnhilde arrive in a boat. The latter's horror at discovering Siegfried with Gutrune is unbounded. She cannot understand how the ring, so lately torn from her finger, is upon his hand. Gunther cannot explain, and Brünnhilde realizes she has been deceived and denounces Siegfried. He, still forgetful of all the past, swears he has been faithful to Gunther, and presently leads Gutrune into the hall, followed by all the men and women. Brünnhilde, Gunther, and Hagen are left alone. Hagen comes up to Brünnhilde and tells her he will help her to revenge. He learns from her that Siegfried's only vulnerable place is his back—that never would be turned to a foe. "There," says Hagen, "shall he be speared." It is arranged that on the morrow Siegfried shall be brought back from a hunting expedition, dead, as though killed by a boar. As they turn towards the hall the bridal procession comes out, Siegfried borne on a shield and Gutrune on a chair, and the curtain falls.

The first scene of the third Act is a rocky valley by the Rhine. The three Rhine-maidens are seen swimming to and fro. Siegfried enters alone. He has got separated from the hunting party by some chance. The Rhine-maidens ask him for the ring on his finger. He refuses, laughing at their warning of danger if he does not give it up. They disappear, and presently Gunther, Hagen, and attendants come in. Siegfried recounts the history of his boyhood, and when Hagen offers him a drink, in which he has squeezed the juice of an herb, his memory completely returns, and, to Gunther's horror, the truth about Brünnhilde is revealed. Two ravens fly across the stage, and Hagen asks Siegfried if he can read their speech. As Siegfried turns to look at them Hagen thrusts a spear into his back. Siegfried falls and dies. The scene changes while the famous "Trauermarsch" is played. The curtains open upon the interior of Gunther's hall. It is night. Gutrune enters, restless, with a foreboding of disaster. Hagen's voice is heard; he appears, followed by a train of men bearing Siegfried's dead body. Hagen admits that he it is who has killed him, and claims the ring. In preventing this Gunther is killed by a stroke from Hagen's sword. As Hagen advances to Siegfried's body the dead man's hand is raised threateningly. Brünnhilde now appears. She has realized the truth of Siegfried's unwitting deception, and has forgiven him. She orders a funeral pyre to be built, on which Siegfried's body is placed. She draws the ring from his finger, and then taking a torch sets the pyre alight. As the flames burn brightly she is seen to ride into the fire on her horse. The fire grows in intensity; the Rhine swells up greatly, invading the hall; on its moving waters appear the Rhine-maidens. Hagen jumps into the river in a last determination to secure the ring, but the maidens drag him down, appearing subsequently holding the ring aloft in exultation. In the background is seen a vision of Walhalla in flames as the curtain falls.

TANNHÄUSER.*

TANNHAUSER is a German knight-minstrel of noble birth, the friend and guest of Hermann, Landgrave of Thuringia, who lives at his castle in the valley of Wartburg.

The scene opens in the Hörselburg, the enchanted abode of Venus, whither Tannhäuser has been lured by the Goddess of Love. He is growing tired of the enchanting pleasures to be met with there. He sings to her, and implores her to release him and let him return to earth. She endeavours to induce him to stay, but he is inexorable. She foretells disaster for him, but he tells her he will then appeal to heaven. Thunder is heard, the goddess disappears, and the scene rapidly changes to the Wartburg valley. Tannhäuser hears the chorus sung by a band of pilgrims passing down the valley, and is moved to invoke the forgiveness of heaven for his sins. His friend the Landgrave approaches, and with difficulty persuades him to stay amongst them.

---

* First performance at Dresden, Oct. 20th, 1845 ; in London, May 6th, 1876.

He is reminded of his love for Elizabeth, the niece of the **Landgrave**, and this recollection induces him to stay.

In the second Act there is a tournament of bards in the Hall of Apollo, at the Castle of Wartburg. Each in turn sings his lay before the Land. grave and his court. Then Tannhäuser rises, and, carried away by the excitement, sings of the Hörselburg as the only place where love can be learnt. All are horror-struck at his impiety, and would kill him, but Elizabeth intercedes and saves his life, on the condition that he joins the pilgrimage to Rome, there to seek absolution for his sins.

In the third Act Elizabeth is watching the return of the pilgrims. They come, but Tannhäuser is not amongst them. In deep grief she ascends the hill to the Wartburg. Night sets in, and Tannhäuser appears, travel-stained. He tells Wolfram, one of the court of the Landgrave, how the Pope declared there could be no hope of pardon for his sin, sooner would the staff he held in his hand bear leaves and blossom ; and how, therefore, he intends to return to the Goddess of Love again. Venus appears in a mist and claims him, but Wolfram points to the bier, on which Elizabeth is being carried to her grave, descending the hill, and tells him an angel has fled to heaven to pray for him. Venus disappears, exclaiming that he is saved. The day dawns, the funeral chant of Elizabeth approaches nearer, and Tannhäuser, invoking Elizabeth's blessing from heaven, sinks to the ground and dies, while pilgrims enter bearing the Pope's staff, which has budded miraculously—the symbol of pardon for the repentant sinner.

TRISTAN UND ISOLDE.*

THE scene of the first Act shows a pavilion on the deck of a ship. Isolde, the daughter of the King of Ireland, is being brought over to England as the betrothed bride of Marke, the King of Cornwall, by Tristan, his nephew. To Brangäne, her attendant, she confides her bitter feelings, that she should be wooed on another's behalf by Tristan. Tristan, who during a time preceding the action of the drama had slain her lover, Morold, sending his head instead of the tribute due from Cornwall to Ireland, and being wounded in the fight, had been tended by her not knowing who he was, and that when she discovered his identity her feelings of vengeance had given way to love. Brangäne endeavours to calm her, but Isolde bids her bring a casket of magic draughts. She sets aside the flask containing a love-potion, and holds up one of deadly poison. Brangäne is horrified at her mood, as Kurvenal, Tristan's attendant, enters, bidding the ladies prepare for the

---

* First performed at Munich, June 10th, 1865 ; in London, at Drury Lane, June 20th, 1882.

landing. Isolde demands a meeting with Tristan, and as Kurvenal goes out to take the message, she orders Brangäne to fill a cup with the poison. Tristan comes in. When she reminds him of the Morold incident, he hands her his sword telling her not to hesitate a second time to take vengeance for his death. Isolde says, " No, drink rather with me, and let our strife be ended." Brangäne, however, has substituted the love-potion for the death-draught, and as the two drink they find themselves over-mastered by passion, and meet in a long embrace as the shouts of the sailors announce the arrival of the ship.

The scene of the second Act is a garden outside Isolde's chamber. Isolde is awaiting Tristan. She cannot give the signal for his approach, the extinguishing of a torch, until she no longer hears the sound of the horns of Marke's hunting party. Isolde presently declares she hears nought but the sound of running water, and disregarding Brangäne's warning of treachery from Melot, one of the king's attendants, puts out the torch, telling Brangäne to keep watch without. Tristan enters, and a love duet ensues. Twice is Brangäne's voice heard warning the lovers that night gives way to day. The duet is interrupted by Marke, Melot, and followers coming in in hunting array. Melot has betrayed Tristan to the king. Marke's sorrowful upbraiding of Tristan's dishonour is only answered by the latter turning to Isolde and asking her if she will follow him to death. As he bends over her to kiss her Melot starts forward, drawing his sword ; Tristan draws his, but allows his guard to fall, and is wounded, sinking back into the arms of Kurvenal as the curtain falls.

The scene of the third Act is the garden of Tristan's castle in Brittany. As the curtain rises Tristan is lying unconscious on a couch, Kurvenal in attendance. The sound of a melancholy air is heard, played by a shepherd. Kurvenal is anxiously awaiting the arrival of a ship with Isolde on board, for whom he has sent. The shepherd promises to play a merrier tune once the ship is sighted. Tristan wakes from sleep, and Kurvenal explains how he brought him back wounded to his old home, and, furthermore, has sent for Isolde. Tristan's excitement is quelled by the melancholy sounds of the shepherd's pipe, indicating no ship can yet be seen. Presently the shepherd is heard playing the promised cheerful air. The ship is in sight. In his excitement Tristan tears off the bandages from his wound, and sinks back into Isolde's arms, who arrives only in time to receive his dying " Isolde ! " As she is bending over his lifeless body, another ship arrives with Marke on board. Kurvenal hastily prepares to defend the castle, but is easily overpowered and is slain. Then, when too late, Marke explains he had come to pardon, for, as Brangäne says, the secret of the love-potion has been made clear. But Isolde is profoundly oblivious of all, and as she sings her death-song over Tristan's body, the curtain falls.

WEBER.

CARL MARIA VON WEBER was born at Entin, in the Duchy of Holstein, Dec. 18th, 1787. When nine years old he commenced taking lessons in music of an excellent master, who lived at Hildburghaussen, named Hensckel. His next instructor was Michael Haydn, brother of the celebrated composer. In 1798 Weber went to Munich, and there took lessons on the pianoforte of Johann Nepomuk Ralcher, court organist, and in singing of an Italian master, named Valesi. While under their tuition he composed his first dramatic work, entitled "Die Macht der Liebe und des Weins." His next operatic production was "Das Wald-mädchen," which was played in Munich for the first time in November, 1800, Weber being then but thirteen years old. In 1801 he composed his opera "Peter Schmoll und Seine Nachbarn," which was performed the same year at Augsburg. At the commencement of the year 1803 Weber met Vogler at Vienna, and studied under him for two years. At the end of that period he accepted the situation of conductor of the orchestra at Breslau. In 1809 he settled in Darmstadt, and while there wrote the opera "Abou Hassan," which was produced in the spring of 1811. From 1813 to 1816 Weber conducted the music at the German Opera, Prague. On Oct. 25th, 1823, his opera "Euryanthe" was produced at Venice. In 1824 he received an order to write an opera for Covent Garden Theatre, and for this he selected the subject of Oberon. He arrived in London on March 6th, 1826, being then in bad health. He was found dead in bed, on June 5th, 1826, in the house of Sir George Smart, with whom he was staying in London.

DER FREISCHÜTZ*

THE scene of this opera is laid in Bohemia. There has been a shooting match in front of the village inn, at which a peasant, Kilian, has carried off the prize the first day, much to the chagrin of the huntsman, Rodolph, the Max of other versions, who is in love with Agatha, daughter of

---

* Was written at Dresden during the years 1819 and 1820, and was first performed at the Theater Königstadt, Berlin, on June 18th, 1821. Weber personally conducted a selection from it at Covent Garden Theatre, London, on March 8th, 1826, two days after his arrival from the Continent. Its first complete performance took place in London two years earlier on July 23rd.

Cuno, a chief ranger, and to whom Agatha has been promised as his bride, on condition that he wins the prize at the shooting match. It is suggested to Rodolph by Caspar, his brother huntsman, that to ensure his success he should seek the aid of the demon hunter, Samiel, who, according to the popular legend, will supply him with magic bullets, which infallibly hit the mark, provided he barter his soul in exchange for them. Caspar has already put himself in Samiel's power, and is bound by the compact to furnish the demon with another victim or forfeit his own life. Rodolph is persuaded to accompany Caspar to the Wolf's Glen, where the seven bullets are to be cast for Rodolph. While, on the one hand, Rodolph thus places himself under the banner of evil, Agatha, on the other, being cast into despondency by an unlucky omen, as we are shown in Act II.—a picture of her ancestor having fallen from the wall—has consulted a holy hermit, who has given her a sanctified wreath of roses, and warned her of coming danger. The scene ends with a duet between her and Rodolph, in which she is anxious for him not to go off into the forest, as he says he must do. The next scene is the Wolf's Glen, where the magic bullets are cast by Caspar amidst horrible sights and sounds.

Act III. begins where Agatha's cousin Annie endeavours to rouse her from her low spirits by singing quaint songs to her. The evil omens continue for her. The box which was to have contained her bridal wreath, on being opened, discloses a funeral wreath. She, therefore, wears the roses of the hermit for her bridal wreath, and repairs to the contest of shooting.

The second scene of Act III. is an open space by the prince's camp. Rodolph is successful, and is requested by Ottokar, the prince, whose chief ranger Cuno is, to shoot at a white dove flying between the trees. As he fires the hermit appears and causes the dove to fly from one tree to another. By this means Agatha, who was at that moment stepping forward from behind the trees, is preserved unhurt, while Caspar falls a victim to the magic bullet.

Samiel appears and claims his victim, and after Rodolph has obtained forgiveness from the prince for having made the compact with Caspar, and it is agreed that he may be married to Agatha, the opera ends with a hymn of thanksgiving and praise, good, in the persons of Agatha and the hermit, having triumphed over the evil, Samiel and Caspar.

www.ingramcontent.com/pod-product-compliance
Lightning Source LLC
Chambersburg PA
CBHW030848090426
42737CB00009B/1151